SURTSEY
ECOSYSTEMS FORMED

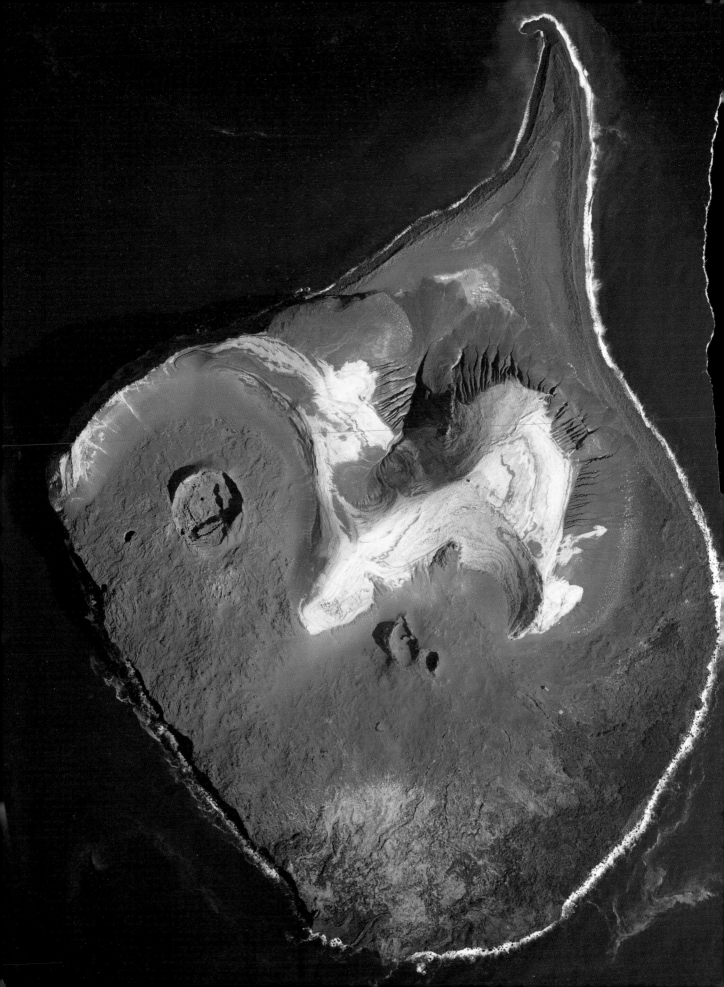

STURLA FRIDRIKSSON

SURTSEY

ECOSYSTEMS FORMED

Reykjavik 2005
Varði
The Surtsey Research Society

Layout Torfi Jónsson.
Aerial photograph by Geodetic Institute og Iceland.
Water color drawing of Surtsey by Sturla Fridriksson.
Illustrations by Torfi Jónsson.

Printed by Gutenberg, Reykjavik.
First published 2005.

Figure on page 2 is an aerial photograph of Surtsey taken at the altitude of 2,000 m on August 12th 2004. On the photograph a green spot is visible, which shows the vegetation of the Gull colony area, Mávaból, on the southern side of the island.

Contents

Westman Islands and the nearest mainland. From a chart of Iceland by Bishop Gudbrandur Thorláksson. Printed 1590.

Preface

This book about Surtsey describes the exceptional event that took place when the sea started to boil off the Icelandic coast. The book gives an account of the volcanic eruption that began on the ocean floor in 1963, and of the formation of the island that, at the time, attracted worldwide attention. The eruption was truly a magnificent phenomenon, to which little else can be compared. It lasted for over three and a half years, and was naturally a wonderful sight for the many tourists who had the opportunity to sail to the island or fly over the volcano.

Of course, as the author of this book I followed the progress of the eruption and the building up of the island with great interest, but I also waited eagerly for the time when the fires would subside and the surface of the island would begin to cool down. It could be foreseen that a unique opportunity for biological research would here present itself, which would be no less interesting than the history of the formation of the island itself, though the former might be slower and less spectacular when compared with the grandeur of the geological story. Of special interest would be to follow the attempt of organisms in colonizing the island

Admittedly, it is possible to study some aspects of colonization by putting out buoys or rafts and then waiting until some forms of life establish themselves there. It also happens that when sandspits form in estuaries, the invasion of life may be observed. But here something quite different and much greater had happened: a whole island had been created, and an extensive area of land had been formed from the primary rock.

From the depths of the ocean there had been built up a broad base, on top of which was an island with mountains and craters, lava flows, cliffs, gentle slopes, flat sandy beaches and withered coastal strips with worn, rounded pebbles and boulder rims that gave the landscape an ancient appearance. Surtsey had thus a diversity of topographical features and a variety of substrates in marine and terrestrial habitats.

Although Surtsey was way out in the ocean, it could be expected that it would not be long before various living organisms began to appear on the island. Some of these happened to fall into a favorable substrate and consequently succeeded in establishing themselves. All such events should be recorded as they occurred, and one could be sure that a trip to the island would always reveal something new of interest to a biologist.

When walking along the coast of the virgin island, it was an amazing sight to see the first leaves of a sprouting seedling like a small green star on the black basaltic sand, the first higher plant to commence growth on this mysterious island. Similarly, it was a great event during an expedition in 1967 when a group of scientists discovered the first flowering plant. The following observation was expressed by one of the participants:

"Walking on newborn land of dust and rocks fresh from the earth's interior is not just another conference field trip. Geologists risking burned noses while bending over the edge of a small crater to get a glimpse of our planet's ultraboiling inside, and botanists huddled down on wet volcanic beach sand in cold rain to see the first plant to flower on the earth's newest mountain are living the thrills that drive field scientists abroad in search of new facts, new ideas and unique experiences."

People have trudged up the track, trodden out in the loose cinders, ascending the hill above the research hut, in order to obtain a good overall view of the spouting craters and the rough expanse of lava. Traversing this lava was slow, difficult and dangerous. There were cracking noises when the newly congealed surface of the lava crust gave way below one's feet, and red-hot magma could be seen glowing in the crevices. It was not advisable to remain long in the same spot, for the soles of one's boots soon started to smoulder, and if a rucksack was carelessly left behind it might start to melt in the uprush of hot air. Bluish vapour arose from the craters, while glowing lava and Pele's hairs were whirled up from the magma mass when the wind swept across the crater openings.

At the same time as the magma poured into the ocean, building up the lava layers one on top of the other, the waves were slicing from the latter enormous blocks that were back-folded upon the edge of the cliff and with fantastic power moving them hundreds of metres along the shore, polishing them into rounded boulders and stacking them up on the leeward side. Sheltered by these boulders, seaweed and seed of coastal plants were washed ashore - the first invaders of life on this newly formed volcanic terrace. The air currents, which blew light pumice around and scoured the mountain cones, also carried spores and feathered seed from the mainland that became stuck in the rough surface of the lava. And one day there suddenly appeared a thin green cover on the black lava-the first moss plants had conquered the newly moulded glassy surface of the rock.

The powerful pounding of the ocean-waves continually broke the rock and carved high cliffs into the lava- edge, and during one spring a few sea-birds found the ledges of these cliffs an ideal place for laying eggs and rearing their young. In this way the forces of destruction and construction balance one another, while the cold, barren surface of the island is gradually transformed into teeming life with green areas of vegetation, swarms of flies and flocks of birds.

Although studies of the life on the island are being steadily continued, they are subject to the whims of the weather. Landing on the island has often been difficult and, although the rubber dinghies powered by outboard motors are excellent vehicles, they have frequently come to grief in the surf barrier. Cameras and various items of research instruments have fallen into the sea, and many a scientist has had a chilly ducking. The sandy terrace has also proved a poor landing-strip for the single-engine plane used for transportation purposes. In later years the transport by helicopter has made expeditions easier. During spells of bad weather there has been no connection at all with the mainland. Yet despite these and other difficulties, scientists have met the challenge and stayed for short or long periods in order to satisfy their curiosity and to trace the history of the development of life on this remote island.

Sturla Fridriksson

1. Introducion

A volcanic island that rose from the ocean floor by showers of black ash, cinders and streams of molten lava in the North-Atlantic off the shores of Iceland made an incredible place of research for biologists. From the island one can see the glaciers perched on their mountain ranges towering on the horizon as a complete contrast to the smoking island, which leads one's thoughts to the dawn of life, to the range life is given between the boundaries of cold and heat, and to the fate of life.

In the old heathen religion of the Nordic Vikings, ancestors of the modern Icelanders, life was thought to have originated as the ooze from the cold world of Niflheimur met with the hot mist emanating from the world of Muspells-heimur. In the beginning there was only chaos, as there was yet no Heaven nor Earth. In the North was a region of snow and ice, and in the South there was heat and fire. And in the yawning gap between these regions, life arose. It was born out of the elements, and although at first hardly to be distinguished from the non-living, it developed into the complex forms of life, with its plants and animals, including man. In the Eddic poem of Völuspá, which was probably written in Iceland in the middle of the tenth century, Vala, the giantess prophetess, describes the birth of life and its fate. She tells Odin, the chief of the gods, about the world tree, the Ash Yggdrasill, about life that was created and developed on earth but in the end would be destroyed in the fires brought by the giant Surtur the black, ruler of fire.

"Surtur fares from the South
with the scourge of branches.

The sun turns black,
earth sinks in the sea.
The hot stars down
from Heaven are whirled.
Fierce grows the steam
and the life-feeding flame.
Till fire leaps high
about Heaven itself."
(Völuspá)

In Iceland the Norsemen became acquainted with volcanic activity, which they undoubtedly connected to the actions of the fire-giant. The Christian Satan later inherited this power during the Middle Ages, and one of the greatest and most active of Icelandic volcanoes, Mt. Hekla was believed to be the main entrance to Hell.

When in 1963 fires started burning from the bottom of the ocean and building up a cinder cone, it was found appropriate that the island formed should be named Surtsey, the island of the fire-giant Surtur.

As by the spring of 1964 it was apparent that the newborn island would survive the destructive forces of the ocean, it started to interest biologists. By conducting biological studies on Surtsey, researchers are dealing with the uttermost outposts of life. It is there that one may learn how life can disperse, develop and prosper on formerly lifeless, barren and dry lava or black sand and beside the boiling vapours of the fissures and vents in the surface of Surtsey. The progress on Surtsey can be compared with the development of life on glacial nunataks, barren peaks that protrude from the ice, or on barren patches of land recently released by a retreating glacier. These conditions are all available in Iceland and comparative studies on such areas could therefore become a research project for scientists on Surtsey.

The emergence of a new volcanic island is a spectacular and a rather unusual event, and it is a unique experience for a scientist to get the opportunity to witness the labor of Mother Earth and to be allowed to watch Nature as midwife dress the newborn with the garments and ornaments of Flora and Fauna.

During the history of man, it is known that only a few volcanic islands have been formed. These events have not been utilized for a thorough and continuous scientific study, and most of these islands disappeared back into the sea.

On Krakatoa, an island in Indonesia, which erupted in 1883, destroying all life on the island, little is known of the first steps in reintroduction of its biota, as the first botanist arrived there three years after the event. At the time he collected over thirty different species of plants. Ten years later the island was covered in vegetation, predominantly savanna and isolated shrubs. On Krakatoa there was no investigation as to the kind of habitat in which each species lived and in what frequency it occurred. Since the 1930´s a new volcanic island, Anak- Krakatoa, has been slowly rising from the sea, and the progress of life there is being more intensely monitored than on Krakatoa. Although the two volcanic islands, Surtsey and Krakatoa, are similar in composition and shape, it is difficult to compare the biota of the two.

Compared with the luxurious vegetation and animal life of the Indonesian neighborhood of Krakatoa with its favorable climate for development of the various life forms, Surtsey is situated in rather barren surroundings with a harsh climate and hostile growth conditions. All developments are therefore rather slow and Nature's effort to bring her garments to the island from her rather poor supply is repeatedly hindered.

Surtsey is the outermost of a group of islands. It is subjected to strong winds that blow the ash and pumice back and forth over its surface, scouring away the attempts of any bold colonist. The Atlantic waves constantly pound on the pedestal, erode the shoreline and pour showers of brine over the island. During the formative period of the island new fissures repeatedly erupted fresh

Fig. 1.1 Landing on the northern shore of Surtsey.

lava and ashes over the island, thus destroying the life already established there.

The colonization of Surtsey is thus like a slow-motion picture that can be followed in detail, but Nature has all the time she needs for doing the job, which she will eventually succeed in doing, and Nature is in no hurry to have this task completed.

The eruption, which began the 14th of November 1963 in the ocean south of the Westman Islands off the coast of Iceland, gradually built up an island, which attained a height of 172 meters and an area of 2,7 sq. km. Half of the area is now covered with lava, the remainder being mostly ashes, which is slowly hardening into tuff, while in places the beach consists of sand and gravel. Geologists, observing the creation of the island noticed seagulls resting on the still warm cinder cone during lulls in the eruption.

The first life forms to invade Surtsey were undoubtedly various microorganisms carried by air and ocean.

My first visit to the island took place on May 14. 1964, six months after the eruption started, at which time various strains of bacteria and a few moulds were collected on agar plates. One fly,

Diamesa zernyi, and a few sea-gulls, waders and a snow bunting were seen using the island as a stop over. In addition, a few plant-parts and seeds of various beach and sand plants had drifted upon the eastern shore of the island. Since then records of the colonization of the dry land biota have been made at various intervals. During the summer months regular observation have been made, but these have been less frequent or completely suspended during the winter months, especially as landing on the island is extremely difficult and biological activities in general are at a minimum in these northern regions. (Fig. 1.1)

The Surtsey Research Society

Shortly after the island was formed and living organisms were discovered on Surtsey it became apparent that those scientists who were interested in Surtsey and its development, would have to organize their research on the island. An excursion to the island was a major undertaking, as it was necessary to use large transport vehicles, ships and planes with specific equipment to be able to land on the island. (Fig 1.2.) The cost of travelling to the island was so great that without cooperation between research teams, the study on the island might have been brought to a standstill. Also a shelter and on site research facilities were needed (Fig. 1.3). Aside from this it was important to collect data and research conclusions for publishing. For this purpose the Surtsey Research Society was founded. In the charter of the society its main purposes are stated as follows:

The purpose of the Society is to promote research in geological and biological sciences connected to the island of Surtsey and in Iceland in general. The Society itself shall not undertake scientific research, but shall endevour to promote and coordinate scientific research in the fields of geology and biology.

The Surtsey Research Society has from its conception rendered valuable services by acting as a centre for Surtsey research. It publishes in the proceedings of the Society results of the projects undertaken on the island. The Society has on two occasions built huts with research facilities on the island, where scien-

Fig. 1.2 Helicopters have been of great help undertaking the transport back and forth to Surtsey.

Fig. 1.3 Pálsbær. The latter of two huts erected on Surtsey, situated by the Eastern Cone, Austur Bunki.

tists on expeditions to the island can stay for short periods of time. Over the summer months during the first few years of the island one or two students of natural sciences occupied the hut. They conducted daily measurements, as well as acting as caretakers of the island. In later years the hut has been used for shorter stays of various scientists.

Conservation Measures

Surtsey was a unique geological phenomenon and at the same time a place that created an exceptional opportunity for biological research. However, to be able to observe the sequence of events on the island it was necessary to make sure that man himself had as little influence there as possible. It was realized that visitors had to be particularly careful not to engage in any activity that would affect natural dispersal of living organisms to the island, or that would in any way alter the habitat and life on the island. Thus it was obvious that in order to secure the natural distribution of life on Surtsey, restrictions would have to be placed on the movement of visitors to the island.

This was a very controversial point, as the island held considerable attraction to tourists. Despite this Surtsey was declared a protected area for the sake of science and tourists have not had free access to the island.

The Icelandic Nature Protection Council had Surtsey declared a nature preserve in 1965. In a press release from the board the Council mentioned that the Surtsey Research Society should supervise the island and that humans were forbidden to land there except with the expressed approval of the Society. It also declared that it was forbidden to remove anything from the island, and import living animals, plants, seeds or plant parts; leaving any refuse was also forbidden.

It was realized that a number of biologists were interested in Surtsey research. Specialists had to be contacted in order to cover the various fields of biological sciences, and coordination of research was needed. The Surtsey Research Society and its scientist members arranged all this.

In the autumn of 1964, the Surtsey Research Committee, the precursor to the Research Society, drew up a priority program for all the Surtsey research. It was suggested that the oceanographic and marine biological research should be handled by scientists from the Department of Fisheries at the University Research Institute of Iceland, both during their regular trips to the fishing grounds around Surtsey as well as during special trips to the island. Regarding terrestrial biology, the main purpose of it would encompass the study of the spreading abilities of various insect species and how their societies would develop; and it was clear that the study of invertebrates would call for the close cooperation of many specialists in this field. Special attention to ornithological studies and the role of birds in transporting other life forms to the island was also required.

Regarding the study of terrestrial flora, emphasis was placed on the dispersal of plants, as rather little is known about the dispersal over sea and by ocean in these northern latitudes. It was realized that Surtsey provided a special opportunity for the study of plant succession from the very first stages, this was also regarded as a long-term project.

The Scientists

A group of Icelandic scientists forms the nucleus of the Surtsey research team. They have organized most of the data collection and the various recordings performed regularly by the guardians and students stationed on the island. However, experts from other countries were also invited to take part in specific studies. Various grants enabled the Surtsey Research Society to obtain the services of competent foreign experts for those research tasks, which the Icelandic scientists have not been able to handle.

Surtsey has thus, in many ways, become an international research center. Alongside the Icelandic scientists in the field of biology, a team of entomologists from Sweden and a team of marine biologists from Denmark, one limnologist and a microbiologist from Germany, an algologist and a geneticist from France took part in the research work. Furthermore, both British and American scientists have been engaged in various fields of geology, geochemistry, geophysics as well as biology on the island.

The unique opportunity for research has enabled many scientists to investigate special subjects, which Surtsey has provided. On the island was a barren territory, completely devoid of life, like a part of a dead moon. It was not surprising that astronauts became interested in a visit to the island. There it was possible to study the first signs of life, to ascertain what forms of life were the most likely to be carried by men, and which living organisms would be able to settle on the completely sterile lava and pumice dust. The results of the research on Surtsey might even give some clues as to what precautions should be taken to prevent the contamination of other planets. It might even be possible to compare Surtsey with some areas in which life has been destroyed; for example, regions that have been affected by nuclear radiation or fall-out. On Surtsey it would be possible to follow in stages how life would re-inhabit and colonize such areas, specifically in the far north, and finally cover the land with life. By noting these stages one could derive knowledge that might be helpful in re-vegetation programs.

In the beginning, the volcanologists were most interested in studying the constructive forces that made the island (Fig. 1.4). Later the scientific emphasis shifted from geology to biology. Exobiologists and microbiologists were most eager to study the thermal sites and other extreme environments. They in turn paved the way for scientists of the many sub-disciplines of ecology.

Fig. 1.4. The viscosity of the magma measured.

2. Geological notes

In the beginning
not anything existed
there was no sand nor sea
nor cooling waves

(Völuspá)

In the beginning, there was no sand, there was no island. For a long time there had been no volcanic activities in the ocean south of Iceland. Nobody expected an eruption out at sea, and there was no warning or a prelude to this incident that could have been a definite indication of an eruption. However, volcanic activity is not an unusual phenomenon in Iceland.

On average there is a volcanic eruption in Iceland every fifth year. Thus there have been over 200 eruptions in the last 1100 years that span the historic era of Iceland. Ten to fifteen thousand years have elapsed since Iceland was relieved of the glacial dome covering the country during the last glaciation, and during this postglacial period, at least 150 volcanoes have been active.

This, however, is not an exact figure, as it is very difficult to be precise in evaluating what can be counted as one crater. A 20 or 30 kilometer long fissure might suddenly crack open, emitting lava from various centers, and build up a row of up to 130–140 craters during a single eruption, as in the Laki crater row in 1783 from which lava flooded over an area of 580 sq.km. Some of these craters might later unite with the progress of the volcanic activity or during a later eruption in the same fissure.

It is hard to calculate the number of craters formed during the Ice Age, when a glacier covered Iceland. During the last Ice Age, i.e. in the Pleistocene epoch, few volcanoes were able to break through the glacial dome and movement of the ice has obscured many of the volcanic centers formed during that period. The volcanic activity that took place under the glacier did not produce the usual form of lava. Emerging magma under-goes a rapid cooling when it reaches the water from the melted ice. It then splits up into small particles of ash, pops up into pumice or rolls out in lava tongues and intrusions, that crack up when cooled and solidify rapidly into pillars and angular fragments of lava. All these eruption products, which are called tephra, later consolidate, the mass of basaltic glass cements together and turns into the brown vitreous breccia called palagonite.

The eruptions that took place under the 1000 m thick glacier of the Ice Age were as today either from central vents or along fissures. Sub glacial eruptions from the latter type built up elongated and sometimes non-continuous tuff ridges. Those from a single crater piled up a cone, which developed into steep-sided mountains capped with layers of lava.

When such an eruption starts under a glacier, the ice is in the beginning melted above the vent and a lake is formed within the ice. As the eruption progresses, pillow lava and cinder are piled up within the lake, which is dammed up by the ice wall on all sides. The enveloping ice also hinders the spreading of the tephra, which is stacked up and may eventually reach above the water surface or even above the glacial dome. When the extruding magma no longer comes into contact with the cooling water, viscous lava starts flowing and consolidating into a flat or convex shield on top of the tuff cone. After the retreat of the glacier the mountain stacks are left protruding high above the plateau, which was previously the old foundation of the glacier. Such mountains now characterize

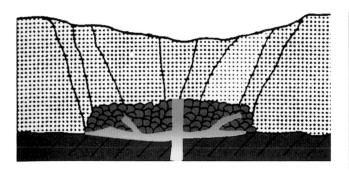

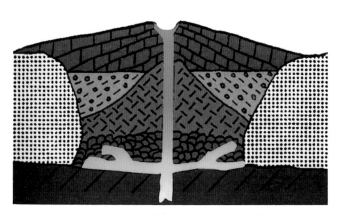

Fig. 2.1. Formation of a table mountain. A schematic drawing showing the building of a table mountain „Stapi" in a glacier.

the central part of Iceland and are known as table-mountains. Volcanic activity in the ocean or lakes is subject to the same forces as under glaciers. During the eruption in Surtsey the theory of how these table-mountains are formed was confirmed. If the ocean would retreat from the Surtsey area what would be left is a mountain similar to the table-mountains of the highlands (Fig. 2.1).

During interglacial periods in the median region of Iceland the volcanic activity, which in all likelihood continued on the same scale as when covered with ice, did not pile up into tuff stacks, but produced lava flows forming a flat volcanic cone or shield volcanoes. Thus there is a great difference in the topography of volcanic areas, depending on the conditions during eruptions, whether sub glacial, submerged in water or aerial.

The oldest bedrock found in Iceland is built up by lava flows from the so-called central volcanoes, which were active before the Ice Age. In these areas the bedrock is never older than 16 to 18 million years. This juvenility is an outstanding feature of the landscape that shows the barren slopes of volcanoes, the open lava fissures and tectonic faults, and the many rough lava flows, as well as hot pools of varying temperatures.

It is known that geothermal activity and geysers are not confined to the dry land alone. Hot water flows out at the shores and has even been recorded on the ocean floor off the coast of Iceland. Thus it is obvious that the volcanic activities extend across the country and beyond it, both towards the north and the south.

Legend 1) basaltic foundation. 2) glacier with crevasses. 3) melt-water. 4) pillow lava with a dyke and an intrusion layer. 5) tephra (palagonite tuff). 6) slanting breccia. 7) lava formations. 8) scree. (Drawings and explanations Th. E.).

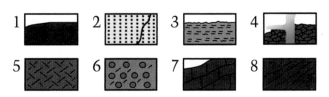

3. The Mid-Atlantic ridge

The median zone of Iceland is a volcanically active belt, which runs across the center of the country from south-west to north-east, covering about 40% of the total area of Iceland. This area has been geologically active for over 3 million years, during the Quaternary Period.

This belt is actually a part of the Mid-Atlantic Ridge that runs through the middle of the floor of the Atlantic Ocean north from Jan Mayen in the Arctic across Iceland through the Azores and Tristan da Cunha south to Bouvet Island in the Antartic, and is a part of a much larger system of ridges and rifts that mark the contours of the tectonic plates.

These plates are in constant movement, and over periods of millions of years have moved several hundred kilometers, tearing asunder the Eurasian and African plates from the American and Australasian plates in the Atlantic, and colliding in the Pacific. The Atlantic ridge is widening, pushing the American plate to the west, away from the Eurasian plate at the rate of 1 cm a year to each side. Iceland is one of the places where this movement can be measured (Fig. 3.1).

A number of eruptions have occurred along this Atlantic Ridge in latter years, such as those of the Icelandic volcanoes Hekla in 1946 and Askja in 1961. An eruption occurred on the island of Fayal in the Azores in 1957 and in Tristan da Cunha in 1961, Surtsey 1963, on Jan Mayen and Hekla in 1970, and in Heimaey in 1973. Hekla also erupted sporadically in the 80´s and 90´s, Krafla also erupted several times in the years from 1975-84. Sub-glacial eruptions happened in Grimsvötn in Vatnajökull, the largest glacier in Iceland in 1983-4 and again in 1998 and 2004. Therefore, whenever the Midgard Serpent wriggles, action may be expected in one of its humps.

Loki had three children by the giantess in Giantland called Angrboda (Boder-of-sorrow), the first was the wolf Fenrir, the second Jörmungandur- that is the Midgard Serpent- and the third Hel.

.... And when they came to him (All-father), he flung the serpent into the deep sea which surrounds the whole world, and it grew so large that it now lies in the middle of the ocean round the earth, biting its own tail....

(The Deluding of Gylfi)

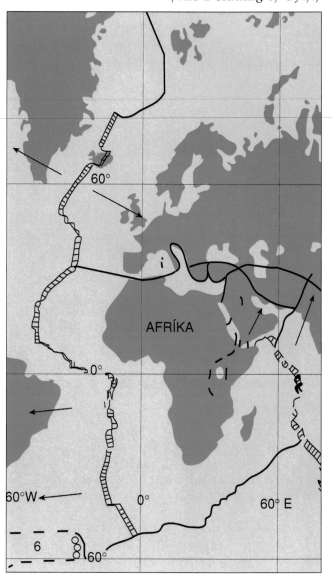

Fig. 3.1. The Atlantic ridge is a fracture on the earth's crust It is a boundary between plates that are drifting apart.

The active volcanoes mentioned above are all situated on points of the ridge system that appear above the ocean, though volcanic activity may also take place anywhere along the ridge. Such eruptions may go undiscovered and unobserved at great ocean depths, as the deep water hinders the emersion of the volcanic activities. Only at the high levels of the ridge or on island peaks are the volcanic activities visible.

Fig. 3.2. Irish monks following Saint Brendan were possibly the first to witness a submarine eruption in these regions, while exploring the northern seas in the 6th Century. From them is this quotation:

„The land is misty, wrapped in stack of smoke, veiled by dark clouds and fog, and the stench worse than from a carcass. Close by is the source of Hell, but the closer one comes, the more difficult it is to locate it. From the bottom of the infernal depth emerges a spout of sparkling fire. With a mild din the wind blows into the embers, but tongues of flames and glowing rocks are thrown so high up in the air, that daylight diminishes. The whole island is on fire covered by smoke, but thousands of demons writhe and squirm, and one may hear screams and groans from the condemned. Oh! Save us, holy abbot!"

Navigatio Sancti Brandani

There may be some controversial problems concerning this rift structure hypothesis of continental drifts and spreading of the ocean floor, however, most agree that the theories are sound. It is therefore reasonable to assume that on the islands the geological features are similar to those on the submarine part of the ridge. Although investigations have been carried out on the submarine levels, many of the phenomena are easier to observe in Iceland. Thus the volcanic activities that took place sub- glacially in Iceland during the Ice-Age may in many ways be paralleled with any submarine volcanic activity.

In Iceland the volcanic ridges run parallel to the fissures across the island, and in a similar way it is known that on the ocean floor there are chains of mountains with peaks reaching a height of 3,000 m and separated by deep submarine valleys. These are mere continuations of the geological formations that are easily accessible on the Icelandic dry land.

As previously stated, the hot water areas exist both on land and on the ocean floor, and occasionally eruptions take place underwater on the continental shelf surrounding Iceland (Fig. 3.2).

Submarine Eruptions off the Coasts of Iceland

By the flat sandy shore off the southern coast of Iceland a group of islands rise high above the surface of the sea. These are the Westman Islands (Vestmannaeyjar), a group of islands and skerries of which Surtsey is the newest member. All of these islands are of volcanic origin and have presumably either been created under ice or in the ocean by the end of or after the last glacial period. Actually, some of the inland mountain stacks on the southern mainland, which are now surrounded by sand, may similarly have been formed by submarine volcanism by the end of the Ice Age, at which time the ocean level was up to 60 km farther inland. Later there has been an uplift of the country, and at the same time alluvial deposits from glaciers and rivers, as well as lava flows have extended the shoreline to the present level.

The Westman Islands were formed in the Prehistoric Era, and although it is stated in the Icelandic Book of Settlement (Landnáma), which was written in the 12th century, that Herjólfur Bárdarson, the first man to settle in the Westman Islands, had built his farm "where now is burned lava", it has been proven by dating the ash layers chronologically, as well as the lava field formed by the stately volcano Holy Mountain (Helgafell) on the main island, that no previous volcanic activities have taken place on that island in historic time. On the other hand, it is known from written sources that submarine eruptions may have occurred off the Westman Islands in the

19th century. It is definitely known that such submarine eruptions have occurred south-west of the shores of the Reykjanes peninsula, where it is possible to follow a submarine ridge way out into the Atlantic. Volcanic activities on this ridge have probably taken place more frequently than recorded, but during the 13th century eruptions seem to have been particularly frequent.

It is stated in annals, for the year 1211, that a number of farms were ruined by an earthquake that struck the southern part of the country. "Then Sörli Karlsson discovered the new Fire Islands (Eldeyjar); the others that had previously always been there had disappeared." It must thus have been recognized that the previous islands had also been of volcanic origin and may have been formed sometime during the period that had elapsed since the start of the settlement of Iceland in 874. In 1226 an eruption recurred off the coast of Reykjanes with ash-fall so thick that day was dark at noon; the following winter was, due to the pumice, named the sandy winter.

Eruptions are recorded in annals from 1231, 1238 and 1246, when the sun turned crimson and earthquakes were frequent. It is further stated that in 1285 some mystical Thunder Islands (Duneyjar) had been discovered west of Iceland, but whether this was in connection with volcanic activities is not known.

These frequent eruptions out in the ocean during the 13th century were quoted in European literature, and many medieval scholars wrote about the natural wonders of Iceland, where both the ocean and the mountains were on fire.

There are no records of submarine eruptions during the 14th century, but in annals from 1422 there is mention of an eruption in the ocean southwest of Reykjanes, and quoting from Lögmannsannáll: "an island emerged which ever after can be seen by those that pass by." In 1583 an eruption once more took place out in the ocean and was observed by a passing merchant ship. In 1783 another eruption started in the ocean seven miles west of Reykjanes, producing an island, which emitted ashes and pumice and made sailing treacherous. The island was named The New Island (Nýey), and the following spring was to be formally dedicated to the King of Denmark to prevent other nations from claiming it. This, however, never came to pass as the island had completely vanished before the official ceremony could take place.

In 1830 and 1879 further submarine eruptions occurred in the same area, but islands were not formed. During the former volcanic activities frequent earthquakes destroyed the outermost skerry, a pillar named Great Auk Skerry (Geirfuglasker). The destruction of the skerry was quite disastrous to the great auk *Alca impennis* that thus lost its main breeding ground. Shortly afterwards this rare bird completely disappeared, and is now extinct.

A description is also to be found of an eruption in the ocean north of Iceland, but although several submarine eruptions have occurred there, only three times have islands been formed and none of them has remained for any length of time.

The Westman Islands seem to have had less volcanic activity than the westernmost side of the ridge. In the Sjávarborgar annals a mention is made of glares of fire being seen south of the Land Islands district (Landeyjar) in October of 1637, and in 1896 fires were seen from land in the ocean south of the islands, but this was not observed at a closer range.

As previously stated all the Westman Islands are of volcanic origin. They consist of a group of 14 islands, excluding Surtsey, and 30 skerries and solitary rocks, made of palagonite with fragments of lava.

The largest island is Home Island (Heimaey), which has been estimated to be at least five or even six thousand years old. Originally Heimaey probably consisted of two islands that were later united by a lava flow from the same eruption that built up the volcanic cone of Helgafell with a circular lava crater at the summit. This is the highest mountain in this group of islands. Later, an isthmus of boulders has in addition united the third island, Heimaklettur, with the previous group and created the island now known as Heimaey. In the eruption of 1973 a new mountain built up to 220 m, which was named Eldfell. With its formation an additional two square kilometers were added to the island, so now it is about 18 sq. km in total size.

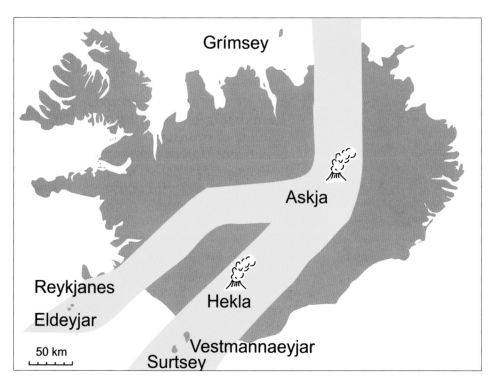

Fig. 3.3. A map of Iceland showing its volcanic zone.

The Prelude

A small trembling of the earth in Iceland is not necessarily an indication of an eruption. Thus no one connected the slight tremor that was recorded on the seismograph in Reykjavík during the first week of November 1963 with the events that were later to take place. It was not known either where the center of origin of this earthquake might have been, nor had anyone paid attention to the slight rise in temperature of the ocean south of Geirfuglasker, which was the southernmost skerry of the Westman Island and a synonym of the pillar that disappeared west of Reykjanes. This slight rise in temperature was recorded by the fishing boat Thorsteinn Thorskabítur on the 13th of November. In a small area the ocean was found to be two degrees centigrade above the usual, but only later was this to be connected with volcanic activities. It is possible that at this point some magma had already started to pile up on the ocean floor. Volcanic activity on land sometimes begins with an increased spouting up of a hot spring, but a submarine eruption needs some time to build up enough pressure to reach through the overlying mass of water. Thus even if some movements had started at the bottom, all was still calm and quiet on the surface.

A few boats were fishing south of Geirfuglasker. Some were sailing with their day's catch towards Peace harbor of Heimaey town. Various seabirds were occupied with their usual search for food in the area. The stately gannets *Sula bassana* with their wide wingspans dove straight down into the deep from high above, while puffins *Fratercula arctica* ducked into the sea from the surface. Perhaps these birds and various members of the rich fauna of these waters sensed something unusual in their marine habitat as the darkness of the November night descended.

4. The eruption starts

*The Midgard Serpent will blow so much poison
that the whole sky and sea
will be spattered with it...
In this din the sky will be rent asunder
and the sons of Muspell ride forth from it.
Surtur will ride first and with him fire blazing
both before and behind.*

(The Deluding of Gylfi)

In the early morning of the 14th of November 1963 the crew of the fishing boat Isleifur II from the Westman Islands had been paying out their line on the bank southwest off Geirfuglasker. When their work completed at 6:30 am, they went down into the forecastle for a hot cup of coffee. Suddenly the crew became aware of a sulfurous smell in the air. This time the cook was not to be blamed, neither was the exhaust from the engine. They searched for a reason, but it was still dark and they could find no plausible explanation.

By dawn the surface of the sea had become unusually rough, the cook who was on watch at that time observed at some distance astern a cloud of black smoke rising up from the surface of the sea. This was not a burning boat, light signal, or oil on fire. No ship had been that close. After watching a black tephra rising in the clouds through his binoculars, the skipper reasoned that this could be nothing else than an eruption of a submarine volcano. He picked up the transmitter and reported the event to the astonished operator at the coastal radio station in the Westman Islands.

Out of curiosity the Captain sailed his boat so close to the scene that there was only half a nautical mile between his boat and the rising fumes. Fearing the increased roughness of the sea and an extension of the activity, the Captain thought it wiser to keep at a safe distance from the column of smoke that was steadily rising higher in the air from two vents.

As the day progressed, showers of ash, cinder and lava bombs thrust up through the air and flew in all directions accompanied by lightning flashes. The engineer on the boat measured the temperature of the sea and found it to be 2°C above normal. The position of the eruption was measured at 63° 18′N and 20° 36,5′W or 5,5 km southwest of Geirfuglasker. At 3 p.m. two original craters had joined and the jets of tephra were becoming more conspicuous. A cinder cone gradually built up from the floor of the 130 m deep ocean.

On the morning of November 15th an island was born, as the top of the cinder cone had emerged above the surface. The pile of pumice insulated the emission of heat and the surface temperature of the surrounding ocean returned to normal. The column of clouds however, rose still higher during the day until it reached a height of 9 km.

During my flight over the eruption site that day, it was noticeable that on the windward side the ocean had a brownish-green color extending only 50 m from the island, whereas on the leeward side the surface was under a constant shower of ash, pumice and lava bombs a few hundred metres out. The brown pumice was floating on the surface and was gradually being carried away by the ocean currents (Fig. 4.1).

On the third day the cinder cone had reached a height of 40 m. The crater, however, was still split open, and during rhythmical explosions from the eruption the water was either thrust out or flooded back into the vent. The wind and waves of the North-Atlantic constantly washed around the new reef as though they wished to

Fig. 4.1. An island was formed as cinder piled up the first day of the eruption.

eject this intruder from their waters. These two natural elements, air and water, fought a hopeless battle against their counterparts earth and fire, which gradually piled up the cinder cone to an ever increasing height. On the 20th of November it had reached a height of 70 m, and by February of the following year it peaked at 174 m above sea level, although it has eroded much since then.

During winter storms the island fought a hard battle for its survival. Repeatedly the ocean waves entered the crater and broke down high cinder hills and pumice ridges that had been built up during calmer weather. With the wind shifting from one side to the other, the entrance in the wall, through which the water could stream into the crater, likewise changed position. As the water came into contact with the flowing magma deep in the shaft of the vent an explosion took place. During such explosions no sound was heard, but a mass of black tephra rushed up and often fanned out into numerous plume-like jets,

which from a distance looked like a bundle or a puff of black feathers turning gray-brown as they advanced into the air. There the vapour was skimmed from the ash particles like a gray fringe of feathers that flew off and joined thousands of others to form the downy quilt of a cloud hovering above the crater. Some of these protuberances reached a height of several hundred meters and were thrust up at a speed of 12 m per second; swayed by the wind they often curved out from the island, discharging the tephra that fell over the edges of the crater or into the sea.

Lava-bombs frequently drove the foremost tip of the feather up into the air and would fall into the ocean, forming a spout of sizzling water on impact.

During this phase of the eruption the ocean was in constant contact with the magma, and a cauliflower column of vapor clouds reached high up in the air, while the ash fell downwind from the island like a black curtain with vertical

Fig. 4.2. Lightnings over Surtsey.

stripes of intense or light ash, depending on the amount of ash produced by the pulsating explosions.

During this period of the eruption lightning was often seen flashing up the ash-gray column. The ejecta from the eruption was highly electrified, the clouds being positively charged. The potential gradient formed was most intense near the crater. After a black jet had been thrust up, a lightning flash frequently followed 10 –50 seconds later, neutralising or lowering the positive charge towards the earth (Fig. 4.2).

Sometimes the ash particles became coated with vapor or ice, which fell down as a shower of rain or hail. Sometimes only a mixture of sea salt and ash fell down as the vapor was released into the cloud. At other times a whirlwind was seen spinning down from the column of vapor clouds agitating the water below, or with the lower end curving inwards towards the island as a result of the centric draught following the updraft of air caused by the volcanic activities.

Most of the ash particles fell on the newborn island or were carried a few hundred metres downwind. However, during intense periods of activity the cloud columns even reached up into the stratosphere and fine dust particles were carried several kilometers or even hundreds of kilometers away.

The distant spread of volcanic ash at high altitude was noticed by airplanes passing across the

Atlantic. Similar ash discharge has since been photographed from satellites, like the 200 mile long ash plume formed in September 1970 during the eruption of the Beerenberg volcano on Jan Mayen. This smoke line contrasted sharply with the cold, dark water south of the volcanic island.

The south-west wind caused ash to fall on the town in Heimaey, polluting the fresh water, as at that time the islanders relied on rainwater collected from roof tops. Later water would be piped to the island from the mainland. Although the eruption looked rather threatening to the neighborhood it did not result in any catastrophic effects on life in the Westman Islands.

The active vents on Surtsey sometimes shifted from one side of the crater to the other, and when finally a relatively secure wall was formed only a moderate amount of water seeped through into the vent. This caused a change in the activities. Pulsating explosions ceased, and instead a continuous uprush of tephra spouted up, sometimes lit up by splashes of glowing lava fragments and bombs. It was a fountain of lava in the making. But as it was still below water level, it was constantly cooled on the surface, so that only ash and scoria were produced.

This phase of the eruption started towards the end of January 1964. Occasionally during such an uprush the vapor clouds suddenly ceased to rise above the water, because the magma surface of the crater was sealed off, while the magma tapped at lower levels flowed through sub-oceanic veins near the seabed.

During one such repose in early February 1964 the most active crater, named Surtur I, completely ceased to erupt. At the same time a new crater erupted farther west on the island. North of this crater an explosion also occurred, probably in early February, forming a depression that filled up with water and became a lagoon, with a small, "All alone Mountain"(Fjallid eina) at its northern border.

After this shift, there was a continuous eruption in the new crater, named New Surtur. A great amount of material was constantly being ejected and thrown upon the crater walls, sometimes hurling lava bombs or fragments as high as two and a half kilometers into the air. By the end of March 1964 Surtsey was a full square kilometer in size.

Lava Flow

The eruption from the new Surtur II crater gradually became less explosive, until on April 4th 1964 when the volcanic shaft obtained a watertight lining of lava and the ocean no longer flooded over the crater wall. When this occurred, the surface of the magma in the vent was no longer affected by the constant cooling of the water and the floating lava emerged above sea level. Lava fountains were formed, spouting 50 - 100 m high columns of glowing magma that bubbled and splashed up from a red-hot lake. All around the lake the lava splashes molded a sort of huge trollish vase, inside which the magma level rose and

Fig. 4.3. The lava crater named Surtungur, seen at night. A pillar of fire rises out of the fountain.

fell with variations in the volcanic activity (Fig. 4.3).

Sometimes the magma overflowed the rim and floods of thin, fiery magma swept down from the crater all over the island, gushing towards the sea with a speed of up to 70 km an hour. This magma solidified, forming a relatively smooth surface of pahoe-hoe or *hellu* lava type as it is called in Icelandic (Fig 4.4).

Fig. 4.4. A solid brim of lava was piled up around the lava crater Surtungur. The pumice cone is seen in the background and the lava apron at right in the photograph.

Fig. 4.5. The lava crater Surtungur was formed west of the centre of the island. Magma streamed from it towards south, where it piled up a hard shield of many lava layers.

Other streams of magma, which ran more slowly, built up a rugged crust like ice in a glacial river and solidified into lava with a rough surfaced *aa* or *apal* lava type. Geologists refer to this stage as the effusive phase. With every new flow pouring out of the crater a new layer of lava appeared. Thus gradually a hard shield of several lava flows was formed over the relatively loose tephra of the cones that had been produced during the explosive phase of the eruption (Fig. 4.5).

The hard shell formed on the loose tephra was as though some icing had been smeared on a devils-food cake. The coating of lava gave the island a hard crust, protecting it from the erosive actions of wind and water.

As the effusive phase of the eruption progressed, a dome of lava was gradually formed. Like wax driblets on a candlestick, magma constantly streamed over the crater's rim and ran down to the sea, sometimes as red-hot surface rivulets, or more commonly in closed veins from which the magma oozed out at lower levels or dripped into the sea (Fig. 4.6).

As the glowing lava flowed through closed veins it retained a temperature of 1100°C, ending its journey cascading off the cliffs into the ocean. When the scorching lava came into contact with the cool ocean steam it was whipped up to form a white fringe around the edge of the island (Fig. 4.7). The rapidly cooled magma formed lava tongues as it ran along the seashore or broke up into small glassy fragments, which were carried along the shore and deposited on the leeward side, forming a sandy beach in the northern part of the island.

By the end of April 1964 the lava crater had reached a height of 90 m above sea level, and for some months the surface-flow from the magma lake was interrupted. Instead it flooded through subterranean and sub-oceanic veins, further strengthening the island fortress against the ocean waves that constantly pounded into it from the south.

During the repose of the surface-flow, the sea-surge broke the edge of the lava, forming cliffs by the shore, and churned up the broken rocks or rolled and polished them into rounded boulders that like the sand were carried over to the northern side.

When the magma resumed its flow from the crater in early July, the magma lake was 100 m in diameter, and from it the magma poured down the consolidated shield and tumbled off the cliffs into the ocean in golden lava falls. These activities continued with intervals until May 7th 1965, but by that time the permanence of Surtsey was assured and a solid lava surface of 1.4 sq. km had been formed on the southern side of the island, and the new Surtur had built up a considerable volcano. This volcano has since been renamed Surtungur.

On August 19th 1966, a 200 m fissure opened up across the eastern part of the island through the old Surtur crater, forming row of small craters from which lava flowed towards the east coast. The largest of these was named August Crater (Ágúst gígur) (Fig. 4.8). This fissure broke through the cinder cone on January 1st 1967, when magma started to flow towards the north. A small crater piled up, Strompur, on the northern face of the cinder cone, later named Austur-Bunki. (Fig.

Fig. 4.7. At high tide the ocean cooled off the newly formed glowing magma on Surtsey. Then vapours rose up at the beach forming a white fringe around the island.

Fig. 4.8. Glowing pillars of magma splashed up through the lava crater, which was formed, when a rift opened on the eastern side of the island on August 19th 1966.

Fig. 4.6. The magma flooded 1100 o C hot in channels or closed veins from the crater towards the ocean. The magma was in many places seen glowing red through cracks in the lava crust as rivulets of magma streamed towards the seaside.

4.9) From Strompur, lava flooded down the cone into the lagoon on the north side of the island, partly filling it (Fig. 4.10). The lava flow even seemed to threaten to destroy the scientists' hut for a while, as it had been constructed on the northern part of the island at the foot of a hill named Bólfell, by the western cone, Vestur-Bunki

The lava flow from the northern crater only lasted a few days, whereas south of the cinder cone the activities continued until June 5th 1967, when lava was last seen flowing from Surtsey island.

Fig. 4.9. Strompur, The Chimney, a crater snout becoming a fumarole that was formed in January 1967. In the background are some of the inner islands and the mainland.

Fig. 4.10. Magma streamed down from the Chimney and filled up part of the inner lagoon and threatened even to destroy the former scientific hut.

5. Formation and disapperance of islets

„The sun will go black,
earth sink in the sea,
heaven be stripped
of its bright stars;
smoke rage and fire,
leaping the flame
lick heaven itself."
(The Deluding of Gylfi)

Parallel with the eruption on Surtsey, volcanic activities took place in the area around the main island and acted like side vents to the main craters, commencing whenever the activities ceased on Surtsey.

Volcanic activity was first noticed on the ocean floor east of Surtsey between December 1963 and January 1964. From the splashing surface lava bombs were thrown into the air, but an island never emerged. This submarine volcano was named Surtla.

From May to October 1965 submarine activities started 600 m east of Surtsey (Fig. 5.1). Similar to Surtsey the activities developed slowly

Fig. 5.1. Syrtlingur one of the satellite islands of Surtsey became 30 m high, but has now vanished.

Fig. 5.2. A column of steam from Syrtlingur. During explosions mushroom shaped piles of clouds were produced.

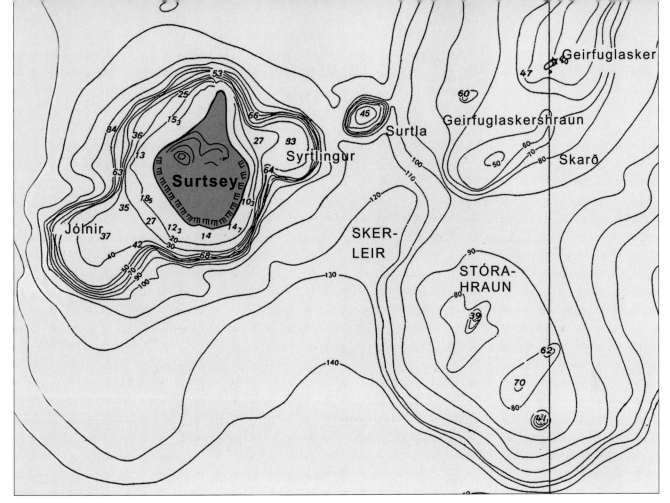

Fig. 5.3. A chart showing Surtsey and the position of the satellite islands Syrtlingur and Jólnir as well as the submerged Surtla.

with waterspouts and emissions of pumice that drifted from the eruption sites. Then the explosive stage that was known from the Surtsey eruption, started and during the fifth day an island was born, named Syrtlingur. The following months the island piled up until it reached a height of 70 m and attained an area of 0.15 sq. km (Fig. 5.2).

During Christmas of 1965 still another submarine outbreak started 90 m to the south-west of Surtsey. Shortly afterwards an island was formed that the eruptive forces had difficulty in maintaining during the winter storms. The volcanological story was repeated once more with an explosive uprush of cinder, ash, and pumice that lasted until August 1966. The vapor clouds erupting from the ocean often reached up to a height of 6 km. The island reached a height of 70 m and an area of almost 0.3 sq. km. It was given the name of Jólnir, one of the many synonyms of the leading Norse god Odin, but it also referred to the island's birth on Christmas day, or Yule.

These two smaller islands were formed just like the pedestal of Surtsey, by explosive activities that piled up a submarine cinder cone, which eventually emerged above ocean level. From their craters floated pumice along to the shores of Surtsey and the showers of tephra thrown up in the air were often swept over the surface of Surtsey, covering areas of the old tuff cone and lava with a layer of ash and cinder up to several feet in thickness. Viewed from Surtsey, these ash clouds often blackened the sun.

Both of the islands were built up of loose tephra. Lacking a lava shield they could not withstand the beating of the North Atlantic. Thus their survival was never assured, in time they succumbed and disappeared into the depths of the ocean. "The earth sank into the sea." Where there once were islands, only shoals remain at a depth of 20 – 40 m below sea level (Fig. 5.3).

Fig. 5.4. Drawings of the volcanically active areas around Surtsey, describing the development of the island. (Based on a drawing by Sigurdur Thórarinsson with additions by the author).

November 15th 1963. A cone of scoria has piled up from the sea floor and an island emerges up through the ocean level.

February 25th 1964. The old Surtur crater ceased erupting, but a new crater was formed farther to the west on the island with explosive eruptions. This crater was named Surtungur.

April 4th 1964. Magma was streaming from the Surtungur crater and started covering the slopes of the tephra cones.

April 22th 1964. The magma floods towards south from the new crater, Surtungur. There a hard lava shield is being created. To the north of the tephra cones a lagoon has been formed.

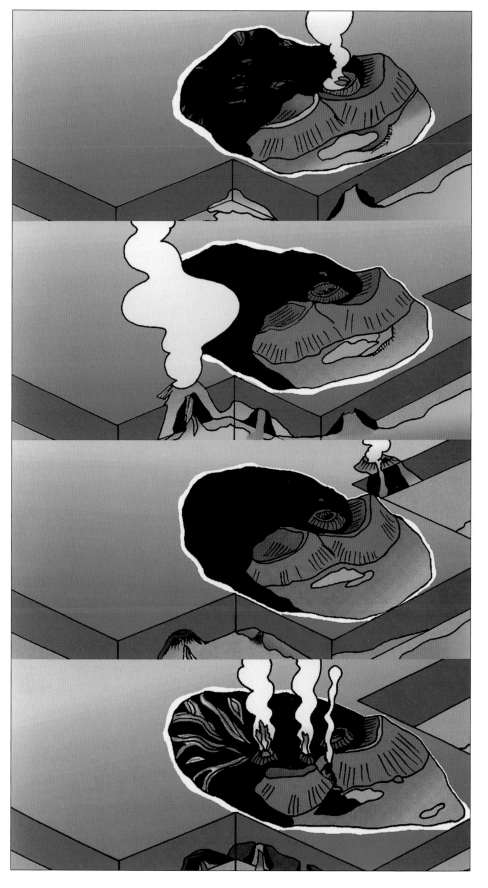

February 25th 1965. The lava crater has been built up into a fountain and from a glowing pool of magma the melted lava streams down to sea.

June 25th 1965. The lava crater Surtungur stops erupting, but eruptions start east-northeast from Surtsey and the island of Syrtlingur is formed.

December 25th 1965. Still another submarine eruption takes place. This time southwest off Surtsey. An island is formed, named Jólnir.

August 19th 1966. A fissure is formed cutting through the eastern tephra cone, Eastern Bunki. A few new craters were formed out of which lava flooded towards southeast. On January 1st 1957 the lava also flooded from the Chimney towards north, into the lagoon.

6. Landscape

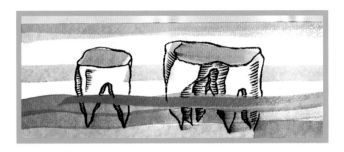

The small islands, Syrtlingur and Jólnir, despite their brief stay above water, markedly affected Surtsey by spreading cinder on its surface. Their fate was the same as of so many islands, that were previously built up along the Icelandic coastline by submarine eruptions. Their activities started on a fissure, and from one or more craters the magma oozed out and piled up into pillow lava on the ocean floor, where the hydrostatic pressure prevented the natural degassing of the material. This continued until the opening of the vent molded by the lava pile had reached closer to the surface.

Near the ocean's surface the hydraulic pressure becomes low enough to allow the dissolved gasses of the magma to explode the material into fine tephra. Therefore, the lava core is not extended any higher unless the activities are long lasting and the cinder piles become so advanced and enjoy such calmness of the sea that a watertight lining of a vent is formed.

In the Westman Island archipelago extensive volcanism has taken place within an area of 700 sq. km. forming at least 60 submarine craters during the last fifteen thousand years that have never emerged or only formed islands that have later broken down. The remains of these volcanic formations are found in submarine lava heaps. The islands we see there today were formed under similar circumstances although they have proven more substantial. It may also be assumed that like Surtsey they were once larger but have been greatly eroded by the elements (Fig. 6.1).

When Surtsey obtained its hard lava shield it was evident that it would be one of the long lasting members of the islands in the archipelago. The volcanic material formed during the Surtsey eruption is estimated to be about 1.1 cubic km, of which 70% was tephra. Only 9% of this material is above sea-level and had formed an area of 2.8 sq. km by the end of the eruption.

Tephra

The two tephra half-moon shaped cones of the craters, old and new Surtur, formed the major parts of the western and central regions of the island. In these sections there are high ridges and hills of cinder and ash with fragments of scoria, or tuff material that is gradually undergoing palagonitisation. The fresh basaltic glass sideromelane started to consolidate shortly after the tuff was produced, especially at the thermal fields. Within a few years it had started to transform into the dense brown palagonite tuff called móberg in Icelandic.

During palagonitisation, water enters the particles and the iron present becomes oxidized, while various elements are lost, such as calcium, sodium, silicium, and aluminum. The ions which are liberated may be found in solution on the glass grains and are available to organisms that later colonize the tephra. The ions can collect together in cracks in the palagonite and create crystals of various formations. On Surtsey ten different crystal formations have been found. Two of these may be new to the world.

The tephra that built up consists of stratigraphic levels with grains of different texture and size, the particles being sorted out by the variation in the force of explosion as well as the wind direction and velocity during the dispersal of tephra from the vents through the air. Airborne grains, however, are not assorted according to size to the same extent as when they are deposited in the seawater. More than 90% of particles of the island fell in sizes between 0.05 to 5 mm in diameter.

The tephra cones reached a height of 174 m and the highest peak on the west of the island was named Bóndi. On the northern and western sides the cones slope down to a level beach; but towards the south they only protrude 50 to 70 m up above the lava shield. As some of the tephra material is still very loose in texture, it is rapidly eroded by wind and water.

On the western side of the island the waves from the south-west and west are constantly undercutting the slope causing slumps and avalanches from the highest hill, Vestur-Bunki. These wave actions have formed a sharply eroded, steep palagonite wall, Vesturklettar that reaches almost 120 m height and is gradually extending towards the inner edge of the western rim of the new Surtur crater. The surf has also sawed out a ledge on the pedestal on the western side of Surtsey. Furthermore, rainwater washes and carries away the fine dust of the substrate to lower levels. Thus the sides of the cinder cones are lined with vertical furrows formed by mudflows that deposit the silt in dumps at the foot of the cones (Fig. 6.2).

The wind also plays its part in carving out the

Fig. 6.1. The Westman Island Archipelago. All the islands have originated in submarine eruptions.

cones, depositing silt at lower levels and spreading it over the lava. The winds blow the tephra about, erode the sides and humps and shear off their surface. When an oval hill, with stratigraphic tephra is sheared vertically, the weathering

Fig. 6.2. The run-off water causes landslides and forms gullies in the slopes of the tephra cones.

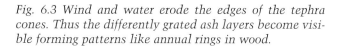

Fig. 6.3 Wind and water erode the edges of the tephra cones. Thus the differently grated ash layers become visible forming patterns like annual rings in wood.

reveals different colored streaks that look similar to patterns in wood (Fig. 6.3). The tephra blown by the wind settles in sheltered places that there either form sand dunes or the volcanic residue is swept out over the island and into the sea.

Lava

The lava shield consists of many sloping and horizontal layers of alcaliolivin basaltic lava formed during the last part of the Surtsey eruption. Although composed of relatively stable material, it has constantly been subject to erosive elements both during and after the volcanic activities.

At the end of the eruption the section of the lava shield remaining above sea level covered an area of 1.4 sq. km, which fanned out over the southern part of the island. With every passing year, the ocean continues cutting down its edges

and is rapidly trimming off the fringes shaping the uneven southern border into a smooth coastline.

At first almost 30 metres were annually sheared off the ledge of the shield. This resulted in the formation of vertical cliffs that reached a height of 5 to 12 m. Now there is an almost 65 m high vertical drop on the southwest coast; on the eastern coast there is less abrasion of the surf.

The lava from the first outbreak was mostly overlaid with cinder deposited from the eruptions of the small islands Syrtlingur and Jólnir. This lava covers an area of approximately 0.75 sq. km, which is half of the total lava cover of the island. The other half was formed by the flow from the August craters, this later formed lava flowed over the old shield in the east (Fig. 6.4). The surface of the lava shield varies in type; some of it consists of the smooth *pahoe-hoe* or *hellu* lava, while the

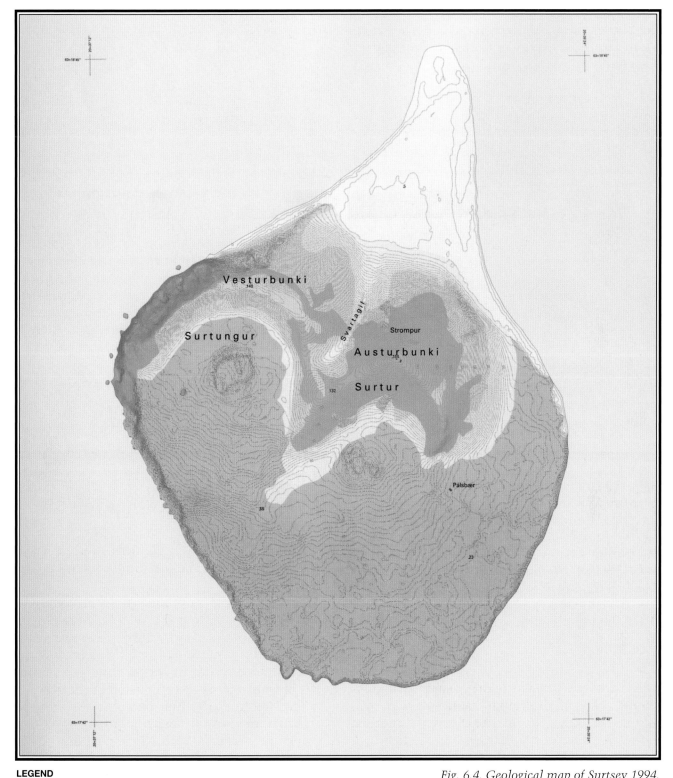

Vesturbunki

Surtungur

Svartagil

Strompur

Austurbunki

Surtur

Pálsbær

Fig. 6.4. Geological map of Surtsey 1994.

LEGEND

- ▨ Lava
- ▨ Palagonite tuff
- ▨ Volcanic cinder
- ▨ Drift sand
- ▨ Coastal deposit

SCALE 1:500

0   100   200   300   400   500

METRES

other type is ragged *aa* or *apal* lava complete with jagged gullies, overhangs and caves. The eastern part of this area has also slowly been swathed in tephra and sand carried up from the beach, blown

Fig. 6.5. A view from The Eastern Cone, Austur Bunki, over the lagoon and the„All alone Mountain", Fjallid Eina.

from the cones filling up the numerous cracks and crevices of the rough lava surface. Close to the cones the lava has thus been almost totally covered with sand deposits, though the lava beds lying closer to the shore still remain quite bare.

Today, about one hectare of Surtsey is lost to the sea each year. The island is now barely over 1.4 sq. km in area and has thus lost 50% of its original size. This erosion is mostly due to the breakdown of the lava, which in many places is porous and unsubstantial.

Coastal Plains

On the northern side of Surtsey there was originally a lagoon protected to the north by a low tephra rim and to the south by the cinder cones (Fig. 6.5). This lagoon has gradually been filled up by silt brought down by mudflows from the cinder slopes or by sand carried in by sea floods or wind; it has also been filled by the small flow of lava formed by the eruption in January 1967. Thus a clay plane has formed in the site of the lagoon. The majority of the material forming the coastal plain, which is the peninsula on the northern part of Surtsey, originated in the lava

beds of the southern part of the island. The lava fragments that are constantly being cut down from the edge of the lava shield are of various sizes and are rapidly being abraded into sand grains, pebbles and rounded boulders up to several cubic meters in size. Most of this material is swept off the platform and brought towards lower depths, but some is transported by the breakers along the coasts to be deposited on the shores on either side of the lava or brought to the northern peninsula.

During the flow of lava in 1966 and 1967 the total area of the island increased, but the abrasion was also great and the peninsula was thus rapidly built up. A new lagoon formed between two barriers on the far northern end, changing the structure of the coast from the previous circular or almost rectangular form with rounded corners to a pear-shaped configuration, which is orientated in a north-south direction (Fig. 6.6).

The surf continually molds the appearance of Surtsey. The shaping-up of the island is caused by

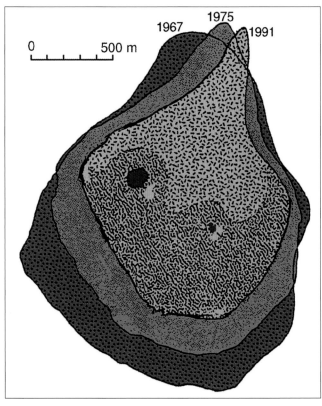

Fig. 6.6. Surtsey has eroded, as indicated by maps of the island at different periods. The island was circular at first, but later became pear shaped, as the sand spit developed at the northern side. The sand spit moves back and forth with changes in sea currents.

the predominant waves generated by low-pressure areas moving from the southwest. The southern part of the island is being eroded and the broken material is brought to the leeward side of the tephra cones. There the peninsula changes constantly. A boulder rim runs along the shore 4–5 m above sea level, extending from the lava edges and encircling the ness. These boulders are well-rounded 0.5 to 1.5 m in diameter and form terraces with sand, gravel and cobbles (Fig. 6.7). During severe winter storms and high tides most of this coastal plain can be flooded and high-water marks are found at the feet of the tephra cones.

Both lagoons have now disappeared, filled up by beach material. The "All alone Mountain" both sea and wind have leveled to the ground.

Habitat

A favorable growth habitat is a necessary prerequisite for the successful introduction of primary plants to a lifeless area. What characterizes the substrate of Surtsey is its volcanic origin. The surface is porous and has a low water retention capacity. Primarily there are three types of substrate; lava, tephra and the secondary beach stratum.

Under normal circumstances soil is produced very slowly in Icelandic lava fields, but the ash layers and sand on the Surtsey lava may expedite soil formation there. This dry and raw blend of surface material, which is devoid of any biological substances, creates rather severe conditions and it will take a fairly long time for flora and fauna to settle there. Fertilizers, brought to the lava by birds, change the surface conditions rapidly making it less hostile to life. Thus some soil formation may soon be expected in the sea-gull area on the southern part of the lava.

The central part of the island is primarily formed of loose tephra that is solidifying and turning into palagonite. This substratum was created in the first stage of the eruption and was constantly mixed with seawater. When tested for soluble minerals, it still had considerable amounts of sea salt. This substratum of the mid-part of the island has remained virtually lifeless.

At first the beaches appeared to be the best habitat for plant life. Organic matter is washed ashore, for example algae and driftwood, as well as the remains of various marine organisms. These organic substances mix with the weathered volcanic ash, crushed rocks, and sand and slowly break down. A great number of sea-birds come to the beach regularly supplementing the organic content of the sand with their excreta. This early stage of soil formation on the beach, however, is very unstable. The rough seas during the winters cause a great deal of disturbances, so that the sediments are churned up, thus constantly changing the stratification of the substrate.

Those nutrients, which are most soluble, are washed away, while others are buried underneath the sand and gravel. Although a substantial amount of organic matter is lost in this manner the sea makes up for it with fresh supplies of drift materials. This cycle is repeated annually, so there are no chances for stable soil-formation. However, some of these organic materials are carried from the beach, above the highest tide-marks and there create a foundation for more permanent soil with an improvement in water retention capacity. Now, these circumstances are found on the northern peninsula of Surtsey.

Fig. 6.7. Boulder rims run along the shore on the spit at the northern side of Surtsey. They are built up of well rounded boulders of various sizes that have been broken off the lava edge in the south and transported by the breakers.

Thermal Areas

Although it was generally considered that the eruption in Surtsey terminated on June 5th 1967 when glowing lava was last seen on the island, thermal activity continued. In 2004 when this was written, there were still high temperature spots on the island. The locations of thermal areas were originally detected by thermal infra-red imagery surveys. In addition, more precise temperature measurements were made on the surface of these areas. The glowing magma in the Surtur crater had a temperature of 1130 to 1140°C. The temperature of magma flowing in a subterranean channel was once estimated to be above 1300°C, while in other veins the flowing magma was measured at a temperature of only 800°C, and even lower temperatures were found in secondary fumaroles and in the cooling lava.

During the three year and seven months period that the Surtsey eruption lasted, it is estimated that the energy generated was enough to raise the temperature of one cubic kilometer of sea by 2°C. However, only a small amount of this energy went into heating seawater, due to the insulation effect of the tephra, but was mostly released into the atmosphere.

In 1970 an overall survey of surface temperature was carried out on the island. The thermal area was found to be mostly confined to the location of the 'primary' energy source at the central craters of old and new Surtur with the exception of an isolated spot in the southern part of the lava shield. In this local hot spot there could have been an emission from a slowly cooling sub-surface lava vein. In the main thermal area heat was emitted from both Surtur craters, but the area between them was also hot.

In the tephra crater of old Surtur heat is still emitted through the interior of the crater bowl. The thermal area extends over the eastern hill, Austur-Bunki, and down the slope on its northern side, where hot steam is ejected from the fumarole named Strompur, Chimney. The Strompur is made of dark lava, and sticks up from the side of the tephra cone by the ravine of Svartagil, which lies between the eastern and western Bunki. From the fumaroles that stand in the slopes of Austur-Bunki, hot steam is also emitted. The western fumarole has been named Ósvaldur, and the eastern, Bjalla. In the western depression, where the lava crater Surtungur is situated, the geothermal heat is more confined to the lava, but does reach into the tephra, where the ridge of the cone has been fractured in several places with many side rifts.

In the lava crater heat was emitted as 100°C hot steam, through numerous fissures and cracks. In a spot on the northwestern side of the crater there was an emission of dry hot air, and in 1970 the highest temperature measured there was 460°C. The hot air ascended from a fissure with a hissing sound. At the southern edge of this crater there was another high temperature centre named "The Grill," where there was an upflow of 200°C hot air, which in places was blown out through openings in the lava with a whistling sound. Outside the thermal areas the temperature at a depth of 20 cm was almost everywhere between 10-12°C.

Geothermal studies were repeated in 1975, and showed that the high temperature area had expanded somewhat but the temperature was substantially lower in the entire area.

In the 180 m deep drill-hole that was drilled for research in 1979 on the eastern part of the island, the highest temperature measured was 146°C. Since then, the island has steadily cooled down, about 1°C annually. Still one may find areas measuring at 100°C in clefts by the Surtungur cone and in fissures in the palagonite.

It is obvious that high geothermal temperatures are mostly connected to the openings of the two largest primary eruption sites; there the heat rises through the tephra and lava on its way out. The temperature drops about one hundred degrees on its way through the damp tephra. However, the heat escapes more easily when rising through fissures and cracks in the lava where it is emitted by hot and dry air. The sea can also easily come into contact with heated areas through fissures in the socle of the island. The sea is heated up when it comes into contact with the hot bedrock and from there steam rises to the surface.

It has been suggested that the slowly cooling pillow-lava that formed the socle of Surtsey during the first phase of the volcanic activity may be generating this heat; and that the heat seeks an outlet through the upper edge of the slanting lava-shield, which is like a tilting lid on a hot pot.

7. Climate

Just as the contrasts of ice and fire characterize the Icelandic landscape, so is the Icelandic climate governed by constant alternation in invasions of either warm air from the Atlantic or cold air sweeping over the country from the Arctic.

Many of the low-pressure areas so commonly formed in the western part of the Atlantic move northeastward and hit the southwest coast of Iceland. As one cyclone follows another and moves across the country, it may carry a warm flow of air causing rain in summer and thaws in winter. During the summer the southwestern wind is about the same temperature as the ocean. When the low-pressure area passes and a high-pressure area grows over Greenland, the north wind starts blowing, bringing polar air with cool and bright weather in the Westman Islands region in the summer or snow and blizzards in the winter.

The climate of the Westman Islands' archipelago is highly oceanic and relatively warm and moist in comparison with the average climate of the mainland with mild winters and much precipitation. The mean annual temperature is the highest in Iceland where measurements have been continuous. During the period of 1961-1990 the average temperature was 4.8°C, and the highest annual average was measured at 5.8°C in 1964. During the same period the average precipitation in the Westman Islands was 1589 mm per year, and highest at 2034 mm in 1984.

Southern and eastern winds are most frequent on the southern coast of Iceland and gales are common. It is often stormy in the Westman Islands; the highest wind speed ever measured in Iceland was recorded there at 111 knots or 57 m per second on February 3rd 1991.

Meteorological data has been recorded on Heimaey since 1872. The weather reporting station is located on Stórhöfdi at the southern extremity of the island. Fewer days of frost are recorded there than on the mainland, only 81.1 days per year in the period from 1961-90. The temperature fluctuations are fairly small in this area. In Heimaey there are also by far the most numerous days with fog for the whole of Iceland, annually 86.3 in the time period.

In general, climatic conditions on Surtsey do not markedly deviate from those of Stórhöfdi. Climatic measurements began on Surtsey in 1967, when a weather station was established by the scientists' hut on the western part of the island, north of Bólfell cone. The station operated only through the summer months (Fig. 7.1).

When observations are compared with those from Stórhöfdi, it can be seen that the mean temperatures on Surtsey are somewhat higher, on average 1°C higher than on Stórhöfdi.

The air temperatures on Surtsey have small daily amplitudes due to the proximity of the sea. This comes to 3 to 4°C on a sunny day and 1 to 2°C on overcast days. The soil temperatures have been recorded at depths of 5 cm and 20 cm. In July the mean temperature of the soil is considerably higher than that of the air. The mean temperature at a depth of 5 cm was 14.2°C and at 20 cm it was 12.7°C. The corresponding figures at Reykjavík were 11.2°C and 9.9°C.

The precipitation on Surtsey is somewhat less than at Stórhöfdi. The records so far obtained show values ranging from 60 to 80% of the corresponding records from Stórhöfdi.

The most prevalent winds on Surtsey are

southeast and eastern winds; rarest are winds from the northeast due to the shadowing effect of the mountains and the glaciers of Eyjafjöll and Mýrdalsjökull. The directions and high velocity of the winds have a marked effect on Surtsey. The strong southerly winds can generate higher waves than the northerly winds, as the south coast of Iceland limits the fetch. In January of 1990 the mean wave height was measured at 14 m, and the largest waves could reach heights over 20 m. For this reason there is a great sea abrasion on the island, specifically on the southern side. The wind and wave action is constantly shaping the island. This can be seen by a comparison of the configuration of the Surtsey maps from various years. Northerly winds are mostly dry, and may carry dust from the mainland of Iceland. During periods of high winds salt spray commonly sweeps over the whole island.

Although the general climate on Surtsey is similar to that of Heimaey, the microclimate may be considerably different, both in the black sand and the various sheltered hollows of the lava. On sunny summer days these areas have balmy temperatures. In spite of high precipitation, conditions are quite arid in most parts of the Surtsey substrate.

No fresh water is found on the island except rainwater in small hollows of rocks, while the lagoons, which contained brackish water, have been filled up both by silt and sand.

Fig. 7.1. A meteorological station by Bólfell. In the distance are Heymaey and the mainland with Eyjafjalla glacier to right (summed in).

8. The origin of life

*"And where the soft air of the heat
met the frost, so it thawed and dripped,
then by the might of that which sent the heat,
life appeared in the drops of running fluid
and became the shape of a man."*
(The Deluding of Gylfi)

Emerging Elements

In volcanic areas on the edges of tectonic plates, the earth's crust is relatively thin and is estimated to be about 5 to 20 km thick, but glowing magma can be found in chambers at a relatively shallow depth under the crust's surface. There the magma is under great pressure and as it enters the surface its various gas components are liberated into the environment. First the gasses are released as small bubbles that later may combine into larger pockets, as the pressure becomes lower with the rising of the magna to the surface. During the Surtsey eruption, the stream of bubbles from the magma through water caused an upwelling of the sea surface in the early phases of the eruption and later produced the splashing of the lava fountains.

The gas that is liberated may differ in composition due to the difference in solubility of the various components and the time of release from the melt. It has been estimated that the magma contains 0.9% water by weight at 1100°C, most of which is released as the magma cools down.

It has been considered of great value if the other chemical components of the gasses could be measured. This was performed successfully during several occasions on Surtsey. The gasses were collected at various sites, such as in cracks in cooling lava where they could be tapped by a tube as they were emitted from a lava stream, or where they escaped under pressure through openings in the roof of a lava vein, or through chimneys or hornitos formed on the solid lava crust above the magma.

The gasses collected under these conditions on Surtsey are considered to be among the purest ever retrieved from hot magma, and they should be considered a true sample of volcanic gasses. The gasses contained mostly water, but also present were sulphur dioxide, both carbon dioxide and carbon monoxide, as well as hydrogen and hydrogen chloride. These gasses included many of the main building units of biological material.

However, the gasses released during the earlier stages of the eruption may have differed from those that were sampled. During the explosive phase the light gasses, which may have accumulated in the upper section of the magma, were presumably released first. In this initial phase the composition of the magma was also somewhat different than at later stages, due to a differentiation in the magma in which the two main components of the basalt tend to separate.

During various eruptions in Iceland a large amount of fluorite has been emitted through the craters with the ash in the early stages of volcanic activity. This was not encountered in the Surtsey outbreak. However, it has to be kept in mind that the amount of sea water coming in contact with the magma was tremendous, so that the low fluorite measurements in the sea around Surtsey do not exclude the possibility that fluorite was present during the initial phase. The analysis of samples of seawater from the Surtsey area, however, revealed that there had been a significant increase in phosphate levels in the sea.

Large amounts of minerals were brought up with warm gases that streamed up from craters and rifts. From these substances multicolored deposits were formed on the surface of Surtsey. They were of varying types and produced diverse and unusual mineral forms, some bright yellow and red sulfuric composites. Most of these

Fig. 8.1. Decorative sulphurous deposits gave the protruding lava rocks a yellowish hue.

Fig. 8.2. Yellow deposits made of sulphurous elements.

deposits were quickly eroded and washed away (Fig. 8.1, 8.2, 8.4 and 8.5).

The fine tephra that emanated during the explosive phase of the eruption may have contained some amount of nutrients, already in a comparatively soluble form. These were likely washed out when the tephra particles rushed through the seawater. A part of the tephra never reached the ocean surface and so nutrients were washed from the tephra at the lower sea levels. Also a considerable amount of ash fell on the island from the column and clouds. Some of the ash was washed and weathered off the island, and thus brought nutrients into the ocean (Fig. 8.3). The high temperature of the seawater bubbling in the open crater further increased the dissolution of nutrients, as did the large surfaces of the small ash particles. During later phases of the eruption the glowing lava flooded down from the island into the ocean, and dissolution from the lava may again have taken place. Thus it was demonstrated on Surtsey that both gasses and various nutrients were released into the environment, a typical result of volcanic eruptions.

In submarine eruptions various types of elements that are available for chemical reactions float through water and air. As a matter of fact cooling magma has released substances into the environment in all eruptions in the history of the earth. Thus the composition of today's atmosphere and salty seas has been consistently building up and changing.

Was Life Produced?

Many have speculated about what conditions may have prevailed on the newborn earth that triggered the genesis of the first, yet simple organic compounds. If we are to simulate in our mind the conditions existing in the cradle of life, we can only rely on some of the natural forces that still exist on our planet. Although life may be a universal phenomenon, a rather uncommon chain of events may be required for its genesis.

The necessary prerequisite for the synthesis of an organic compound is the presence of raw materials in an available form and an energy source that can speed up chemical reactions. The required energy may have been in the form of heat, electricity, or radiation. The primordial synthesis of biological molecules may have taken place in the primitive atmosphere, and later the molecules were dissolved in water or, what is more likely, the cradle of life was in the ocean or a crater lake where the raw materials were found in water solution. The interphase between air and water is a place that makes an ideal environment for linking up atoms. But the chances of chemical synthesis are even greater at the interphase between molten lava and ocean water, where a solution loaded with inorganic nutrients is brought to a sudden boil.

A submarine eruption provides all the possible combinations of elements and forces that might be required for such an organic synthesis. If similar reaction did take place during an eruption in primordial times, why could not the same take place on Surtsey in present days?

An ingenious medieval metallurgist with a vivid imagination would never have dreamed that such a Plutonic atmosphere, as that which hovered over Surtsey, could exist on earth. Just as it will be difficult for today's scientists to imitate all the variables provided in the natural laboratory of Surtsey with its energy supplied by numerous lightnings striking a vapor cloud loaded with suspended nutrients, or the glowing lava sizzling in the ocean broth. During the Surtsey eruption several attempts were made to ascertain whether any organic compounds of abiogenic origin were being produced.

Fig. 8.3. A volcanic explosion in Syrtlingur. The cinder falls like a fringed carpet over the island and into the steaming ocean.

Scientists arrived at the island and collected the new fallen ash carried from the eruption in Syrtlingur. The ash was collected both before and after it fell to the surface of Surtsey. The scientists also sampled dry and wet surface dust from Surtsey and from crater fumaroles, where the temperature ranged from 120 - 150°C. In the ashes from Surtsey some organic matter, amino acids, were found; their presence was extremely interesting. However, it could not be definitely concluded that they were of abiogenic origin. It was possible that the samples could have been contaminated by environmental sources, such as from the ocean floor, the seawater, and the atmosphere through which the ash and gases were ejected during eruption. Still it is worth noting that the amino acids analyzed in the ash were not the same as those found in samples of seawater from around the island. This evidence could indicate an abiogenic origin, of the amino acids found on the ash particles created in the eruption.

Previously it had been suggested that an experiment to create amino acids during an eruption could be performed in such a way that contamination was kept at a minimum. On this premise a simple experiment was performed. An attempt was made to create organic matter by dropping molten lava into samples of water, which had artificially produced, sterilized and bio-substance free seawater of three types, all free of organic substances.

During an expedition to Surtsey on October 14th 1966, it was possible to get access to and obtain molten lava in an isolated opening approximately 500 m from the crater, where the 1100°C hot magma flowed in subterranean veins or closed tunnels from under solidified surface of somewhat older lava. The solid lava surrounding the open fissure was free of any vegetation, as Surtsey was almost devoid of life at that time and there seemed to be little chance of any contamination from the air.

The molten lava was now scooped up with a ladle from the magma stream and poured into three aluminum vessels, each containing a different kind of nutrient solutions in water (Fig. 8.6). Approximately 3 kg of magma was scooped into each container. When the molten lava came in contact with the water solutions an explosive boiling occurred, so steam erupted from the containers for at least 5 minutes. During the sudden contact between lava and water, the temperature of the solution increases rapidly. Should the proper elements for a synthesis be present, the chances are that they might combine into simple organic compounds. And precisely by this experiment it could be demonstrated that the solutions, which had come into contact with the hot magma, contained several amino acids, especially glycine and alanine.

Fig. 8.4. The sulphurous deposits did not last more than a few years.

This and other experiments strongly suggest that abiogenesis does not necessarily have to be confined to the primordial conditions on primitive earth, but rather that a synthesis of simple organic compounds can take place wherever conditions may be similar to those present at that time. Such conditions may exist during volcanic activities, especially in submarine eruptions.

Genesis of life may after all be a more common phenomenon than hitherto accepted. Spontaneous generation may at any time be a frequent and inevitable process on our planet. The fate of the simple organic compound, which may be formed in this way, is not necessarily a simultaneous breakdown, nor is it likely that these compounds will form a basis for an evolution of new organisms. However, they undoubtedly become building material for various organisms that are almost always present somewhere in the neighborhood. It is likely that any free amino acids, which might be synthesized in this way, are instantly attached to larger molecules and used in the life processes by some organisms.

Fig. 8.6. The author scooping hot lava, which he poured into a container with sea water, an experiment to detect a possible formation of organic molecules during volcanic eruptions.

Fig. 8.5. Many lava rocks were covered with the yellow deposits.

9. Ecological aspects

The ash is the best and greatest of all trees, its branches spread out over the whole world and reach up over heavens.

The ash Yggdrasill endures more pain than men perceive, the hart devours it from above and the sides of it decay, Nidhögg is gnawing from below.

(The Deluding of Gylfi)

The biota of various islands differs widely in origin, richness and composition. Distant islands, which may be hundreds of kilometres from other landmasses, are often rich in endemics, if they are of ancient geological origin. Islands of more recent origin are often poor in species and have but a few endemics.

Those, which have undergone recent denudation or have recently emerged from under the ice or out of the sea, are ecologically poorly advanced.

Biologically speaking such islands are interesting subjects and, due to their simplicity in species, are well suited for basic ecological investigation. In the following chapters a few of these ecological aspects will be dealt with that concern some of the biological problems in Iceland, including that of the Westman Islands and the most recent member, the new-born volcanic island of Surtsey. There one may compare the conditions of smaller islands with those of the larger ones, and primitive communities with the complex and more advanced in succession. However, in order to understand the ecological problems on Surtsey a brief account should first be given of some general biological aspects concerning Iceland.

The Icelandic Biota

Most of the Icelandic fauna must have dispersed to Iceland in post-glacial time. The birds, which have been recorded as seen are of 360 species, of which 100 species have nested in Iceland and only 30 species are permanent residents; the others migrate to the south in winter. Of dryland mammals only the fox, mouse, rat, reindeer and mink live wild, and all but the fox have been introduced. Salmon, brook-trout, char, eel and stickleback are found in lakes and rivers, but there are no reptiles, and no ants nor mosquitoes among the 900 species of insects which have been found in the country.

In the post-glacial flora of Iceland there are approximately 460 species of vascular plants. This assembly of species and communities is in accordance with the climatic conditions of the country, which is subarctic to arctic, but at the same time oceanic with relatively mild winters that are moist and windy.

It has been commonly accepted by many Icelandic botanists that more than half of the species in the indigenous flora have survived at least the last glaciation. This element of the flora is considered to have reached the island by a land-bridge, connecting Iceland with the continent of Europe, during the last interglacial period. And that these species survived the last glaciation as small refugia on nunataks and other ice-free regions, while the greater part of the country was covered by glaciers. The remainder of the species in the present Icelandic flora must accordingly have reached Iceland in post-glacial times. This theory is partially supported by the fact that a number of species seem to have a centric distribution corresponding to regions that, according to some geologists, might possibly have remained ice-free during the last glaciation (Fig. 9.1).

An earlier opinion was that Iceland had been completely covered with ice and that all species

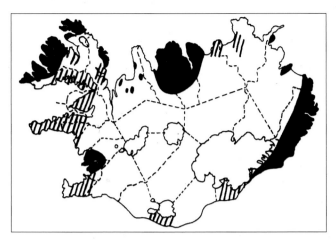

Fig. 9.1. A map of Iceland, showing the centers (black) and possible districts (hatched), where plants may have overwintered in Iceland during the last Ice Age.

in the present biota would have had to disperse post-glacially over the ocean.

At present, it will be difficult to prove either theory. But if it is assumed that half the number of species in the present flora could have dispersed to the island over the ocean in post-glacial time, one might therefore just as well argue that a greater part of, or even all the species, could possibly have come in that way across the ocean.

The Icelandic biota must, for instance, be young in the country, as no true endemic species are encountered. Neither is the centric distribution necessarily an indication of glacial survival. The species may have a centric distribution due to a late sporadic immigration or because of certain environmental conditions at the centric locations, favouring certain elements of the biota there. Thus, in the north central mountain ridge, alpine-arctic species predominate; in the south central region the temperate element is found, and so on. These centres have definite environmental boundaries.

Since the time of the settlement of Iceland over 1100 years ago, man has greatly influenced the vegetation of the country. There were no herbivorous mammals in Iceland prior to the settlement, and the vegetation may be considered to have been in perfect balance with other natural forces at that time. However, with the introduction of domestic animals there was a drastic change in the biotic harmony and an upset of the equilibrium that the vegetation had reached with the environment. Cultivated plants and weeds

were introduced, some of which spread rapidly and invaded the native communities. Ever since, there has been a sporadic introduction of species. Since the turn of the last century, for example, 190 new accidental introductions of vascular species have been recorded. In addition, deliberate plant introduction is made by various gardeners, the Agricultural Research Institute and the Iceland Forest Service.

Many of the introduced species of plants and animals have become well established and may be considered permanent members of the present biota, whereas others are dependent on rather artificial man-made habitats and have only become temporary immigrants. It is obvious that a greater number of species than those that were present in the original native Icelandic biota are able to survive in the country.

The poverty of species is to some extent caused by the recent geological origin of Iceland or recent emersion from the glacial dome, as well as by the edaphic and climatic conditions, the latter being rather selective due to the subarctic location of the country. But the oceanic barrier and the distance from the source of available species must also have affected greatly the quantity of species in the native biota. There are, for example, no plants with burs or bristles that have been dispersed by mammals.

The oceanic barrier as a selective factor in dispersal can to some extent be studied on islands, which have previously been devoid of life. New volcanic islands, such as Surtsey, offer favorable conditions for this kind of research.

Ecological Studies on Surtsey

When discussing the subject of colonization of biota on the island of Surtsey, many interacting factors have to be considered, such as: (1) the location of the territory; (2) the source of available species for dispersal; (3) the means of dispersal; (4) landing facilities; and (5) living conditions on the island.

As Surtsey is an island in the North Atlantic Ocean, it already occupies a special position that primarily limits a great number of possible colonizers of the island to arctic and subarctic species. Secondly, the invading biota has to be transported over an ocean barrier, which again obviously excludes a vast number of species that might otherwise have a chance to colonize the island, for instance, those species that depend exclusively on dispersal by land animals. The colonization of Surtsey is in that respect not comparable to isolated areas on land or areas with similar substrata on the mainland, such as new lava flows or barren sand stretches, where to plants may be carried attached to terrestrial animals, or where to they might be blown by rolling over a land surface, or simply where to they could spread by vegetative growth. The colonizing plants on Surtsey have to overcome greater obstacles and a more selective barrier.

The amount of living material dispersing to Surtsey should be roughly in reverse proportion to the distance of the source of available species. This might, however, be biased by some special and local conditions, such as strong air and ocean currents and the selective long-distance dispersal by migratory birds. Surtsey is a member of a group of islands, the nearest being Great Auk Skerry (Geirfuglasker) at a distance of 5.5 km. It is reasonable to consider this and the other outer islands to be the most likely habitats from which biota could colonize Surtsey. A thorough examination of the biota of these individual islands is thus a necessary prerequisite to such an investigation. Should their individual biota vary in number of species, the survey enables a determination of the minimal distance a species has to be transported in order to reach Surtsey. This again reflects the spreading potentiality of various species.

A dispersal from the mainland of Iceland is also extremely probable, where the vegetation of the southern part has an obvious advantage over the more arctic element of the interior and the northern districts. Finally, there is the possibility of a long-distance dispersal. This would most likely be from other European countries, though America and other sources should not be excluded.

Although the study of the colonization of Surtsey is of great interest per se, it could thus also furnish information on the long-distance dispersal of plants and animals in the North Atlantic basin and give valuable answers to many a riddle in the great confusion and dilemma of the argument between those who believe that all life was completely eradicated in Iceland during the last glaciation, or the tabula rasa *theory, and those who believe that life in Scandinavia and Iceland survived the last glaciation on ice-free centres or nunataks.*

10. Ways of dispersal

When they were going along the sea-shore, the sons of Bor found two trees and they picked these up and created men from them.

(The Deluding of Gylfi)

The major ways of dispersal to Surtsey are by ocean or air. Plants and lower animals can also be carried by drifting objects, by birds or other animals and even by man.

Dispersal by Ocean

Dispersal by ocean is the most likely way of invasion, and obviously the marine bacteria, moulds and algae have the advantage there. However, the seeds and other diaspores of vascular plants found drifted on the shore of Surtsey already make up a long list. As early as May 14th 1964 wilted leaves and stems of *Leymus arenarius* and *Juncus arcticus* were observed in the debris, and seeds of the following species were collected: *Angelica archangelica*, *Cakile edentula* and *Leymus arenarius*.

At the same time green plants of *Sedum rosea* and *Matricaria maritima* were discovered on the shore. A plant of the latter species, which had drifted on to the shore, was successfully kept alive in a pot for some time, which shows that diaspores other than seeds can disperse to the island and begin growing. Similarly, stolons of *Leymus arenarius* can withstand the ocean transport and start to develop on the sandy habitat of Surtsey.

Species common on the neighboring islands are most abundant in the drifted material, which indicates that the distance from source of plant material and its available quantity mostly influences the incidence of dispersal. Thus *Cochleria officinalis* and *Festuca rubra* are frequent in the drifted material, both being common species on the neighboring islands as well as on Heimaey (Fig. 10.1 and 10.2).

Fig. 10.1. A tuft of grass drifted to the boulder shore of Surtsey in 1972.

51

A stalk of *Hippuris vulgaris* must have derived from the mainland of Iceland, as this species does not occur on the Westman Islands. Parts of such species can easily be carried from the interior down the rivers and then drift over to the islands as seeds or other floating plant parts. It is interesting to note that seeds of *Cakile edentula* are found among the debris in most years, although that species does not grow permanently on the island.

The dispersal by ocean to Surtsey is affected by the direction of surface winds and sea currents, by the buoyancy of the seeds and other plant parts and by the ability of seeds to retain their germination ability after immersion in salt water. In order to understand fully the possibility of ocean dispersal to the island it is thus necessary to note the speed and directions of the currents around Surtsey. Having obtained information on such factors it is possible to estimate whence and at what time seeds could drift to Surtsey.

As the general direction of ocean currents around the islands is fairly well known one could predict the course of drifting objects in the area.

The westward trend of the current, for example, moved most of the pumice produced in the Surtsey eruption to the shores of Reykjanes peninsula in the south-western part of Iceland.

Similarly, one would expect diaspores to reach Surtsey by ocean transport from the eastern coast of Iceland or from the islands farther to the east.

The ocean currents, however, are not the only forces affecting the transportation of objects on the sea surface, as this is also highly influenced by wind. During the summer of 1967 an experiment was performed in order to demonstrate the drift which might take place from Heimaey. A few million plastic grains 2- 4 mm in diameter were released into the sea from that island and an observation made of the drift. The winds shifted several times dur-

Fig. 10.2. The turf overhangs the ocean cliffs on nearby islands and some falls into the sea. The photo is taken 1965 in Súlnasker with Geirfuglasker and Surtsey in the distance.

ing this period and were not always favorable for the drift to Surtsey, but finally one week later a few hundred grains reached the island. The grains had thus drifted at the speed of 2.5 km per day. Theoretically, diaspores transported by ocean fall off the edges of the source island, whence they float and drift away in all directions radiating from the source island until their drift is intercepted by an obstacle such as the shore of Surtsey. Should the diaspores float long enough the chances of reaching the shore of Surtsey can be expressed as the proportion between the Surtsey sector and the total circumference of a ring with a centre in the source island and the distance between the islands as the radius.

The amount of diaspores falling off the source island depends on the type of vegetation, on weather, season and probably on a number of other factors, but mainly it depends on the circumference of the source island. The longer the shore, thus more seed and fruit can fall off the island.

There is a variable chance for seed to drift to Surtsey from the various islands. When taking into account the circumference of the islands and their distance from Surtsey, it may be possible to predict the amount of drift to Surtsey. Although Heimaey is relatively distant its effects are great. However, it has to be kept in mind, that the floating capacity of seeds and stalks are limited and that they eventually sink; and it was not known, whether the buoyancy of propagules of all species was enough to allow them to drift from Heimaey to Surtsey. The buoyancy of seed is of value for ocean dispersal, but this characteristic of the seed is not essential for its ability to disperse by ocean, since seeds can float attached to all sorts of driftwood, debris and ice. In that way small animals could also be carried to Surtsey

It could be expected that seeds would lose their viability after lying in salt water.

In an experiment, which was performed in order to determine the survival period of seed in sea-water, it was demonstrated that seeds of a number of Icelandic species keep their germination ability for a long time after such treatment. At the end of a four month period the salt water had produced only minor changes on the viability of the seed, indicating that many an Icelandic species could easily disperse from the mainland by ocean to Surtsey.

The landing facilities on an island are a further problem in means of dispersal. In that respect, Surtsey differs from most of the outer islands in having low sandy beaches favouring the landing of drifting seeds. One would, therefore, expect the ocean route to be the most plausible way of dispersal of seed to Surtsey.

The colonization of the coastal plants that are now growing on Surtsey definitely proves that diaspores have dispersed successfully to the island in this way. Both *Leymus arenarius* and *Honckenya peploides*, which started to grow in the high-tide zone, have later spread to other parts of the island. They are both successful colonizers on Surtsey,

Mermaid's Purses as Dispersers of Seeds

During the summer of 1969 the shores of Surtsey were regularly searched and records made of the

Fig. 10.3. Mermaid's purses, the capsulated eggs of the skate, were covered with seed and had drifted to the shore of Surtsey.

drifting diaspores, but rather few seeds were discovered. It was, however, noted that during May a number of "Mermaid's purses", the capsulated egg of the skate Raja batis, had drifted ashore (Fig. 10.3). When these were inspected, a number of seeds were observed attached to the rough outer surface of the "purses". The chitinous material of the purses was somewhat shredded into thin bristles to which the seeds adhered. Some of the seeds were hairy, which still further increased the adhesive effect. The seeds found on the purses were identified, counted and listed according to species and quantity of seed per purse. Except for one infertile fruit of Carex, the seeds found attached to the mermaid's purses were all of grass species common in Iceland. These were *Agropyron repens, Leymus arenarius, Phleum alpinum*, and *Alopecurus geniculatus*. However, only *Leymus arenarius* is found growing on the smaller islands of the Westman archipelago; but all are found growing on Heimaey, the largest island, as well as on the mainland of Iceland.

It must be presumed that the seeds and purses came into contact on some neighboring coast, where the seeds became attached, and from where they were dispersed to Surtsey. The shortest possible distance of dispersal for this collection of seeds that were attached to the purses is between Heimaey and Surtsey, a distance of 20 km.

It has long been known that fish may eat seeds and thus take part in their dispersal. On the other hand, it has not previously been recorded that fish eggs can also act as dispersers of seed.

Other animals are a further means of seed transportation. Among the mammals, seals live around Surtsey, but it is doubtful that they carry any diaspores to the island. The birds, which frequent the island, are a better means of transport.

Transport by Air

While transport of life-forms by ocean depends upon direction and speed of sea-currents, the air transport varies according to time of year and wind directions around the island as well as climate in the North Atlantic.

It has been demonstrated in Surtsey, that the island is subject to showers of airborne micro-organisms that continuously fall on its surface.

The dispersal by air of lower plants to Surtsey has been measured on various occasions by counting colonies on agar plates. By this route both bacteria and moulds are brought with air currents. Similarly, spores of ferns and lichens will be able to disperse by wind. Spores of mosses are also apparently carried to the island in large quantities, rather from the extensive moss fields of the mainland than from the small moss colonies of the neighboring islands. However, the possibility of transportation of the vegetative parts of moss, although much heavier than spores, cannot be overlooked, as this is a frequent means of spreading of moss over lava flows on the mainland.

Seeds of vascular plants equipped with plumes for wind dispersal have also been noted, for example, once a shower of small fruits of the common groundsel, *Senecio vulgaris*, came drifting on the air like an invasion of parachutists. These fruits very likely came from the mainland rather than from the smaller islands.

Similarly, in the autumn of 1971 and again in 1972 there was an airborne invasion of the nuts of cotton grass, *Eriophorum scheuchzeri*. These must have been carried from the mainland of Iceland, since cotton grass is not found on the smaller islands and the small colony of cotton grass on Heimaey did not produce seed. Only the light seeds and those equipped with bristles for the purpose will be conveyed in this way to the island, and it is evident that such a transport is quite selective towards a limited number of species that are capable of air dispersal.

It has been shown that whenever a flock of migratory birds or butterflies arrived on Surtsey, there were favorable winds for their flight from the continent of Europe or the British Isles. Similarly, an increase in number of insects was noted when northerly winds were blowing from the mainland of Iceland. At such occasions there could be sunshine and calm weather on the southern lowland, but windy in the Westman Islands. Insects flying at the lowland could easily be caught in the updraft and carried out to Surtsey.

Dispersal by Birds

As previously stated, distant islands must to a great extent owe their plant and animal life to

Fig. 10.4. Plastic containers were set up to collect organisms that birds might possibly carry to the island.

In order to study freshwater biota on Surtsey, some traps were set up in the form of sterile laundry tubs. The rain-water gradually filled up some of these tubs, and they were thus frequently visited by birds that used the water for drinking and bathing. After two years of exposure up to 25 different species of lower organisms were found in some of these traps, and there was a green tinge of algae on the sand in the vicinity of the tubs, bird feathers, droppings, and even some vascular plants. (Fig. 10.4) Many of these organisms must undoubtedly have been transported by birds. In addition to these observations on the part played by birds in dispersal of organisms, it was noted that birds carry various smaller organisms and parts of tissues on their feet. Feet of 90 migrating birds, caught after having landed on Surtsey, were inspected for organisms. On thirteen individuals various species of diatoms and spores of moulds and mosses were discovered, as well as filaments of moulds and parts of tissues of higher plants.

long-distance dispersal of living material. The role played by birds has long been in dispute among biologists.

The almost sterile habitat of the new volcanic island of Surtsey offered a unique opportunity to study the possible role of birds in transporting plants and lower animals across wide stretches of ocean.

Sea-gulls are constantly soaring above Surtsey and various sea-birds inhabit or visit the island. Similarly, many migratory birds land there during their flights between Iceland and the more southern countries of Europe or from farther north.

Any of these birds may act as carrier of small organisms and disperse plants and animals to Surtsey. Thus it has been observed that some of the vascular plants that are now growing on the island have definitely been brought in by sea-gulls. In many cases the plants have grown out of bird droppings or their offal.

The birds which have now started to nest on Surtsey carry plant material to their nesting grounds, and can in that way transport diaspores to the island. Their nests then serve as incubation areas for various smaller organisms, which enjoy shelter, heat, and the fertile soil provided by the birds. These spots become colonization centres for such organisms.

Some of the migratory birds caught on Surtsey have had parasites, both in their alimentary tract as well as on the exterior of their body. Beetles have been discovered in their throats and these in turn may also host parasites. Some of these organisms may spread among the local bird population and become inhabitants of the island.

The sea-gulls of Surtsey undoubtedly bring the diaspores from the neighboring islands. When the Herring Gull started to nest in Surtsey there occurred a great increase of new plant colonizers. The birds have obviously carried seeds of various nitrophil, vascular plants from the neighboring islands to their breeding grounds in Surtsey. The raven *Corvus corax* has also brought seed to its nesting site of a sea thrift *Armeria maretima*. Other migrants, such as geese that land on the island in autumn are also capable distributors of seeds, but a long-distance dispersal may also be affected by some of the migratory birds.

Birds and Seed Dispersal over Long Distances

Surtsey, being the southernmost territory of Iceland, has become the first landing place for migratory birds arriving in the spring from European countries. Thus, migration of birds to the island was recorded and a variety of birds were collected on Surtsey as they arrived. These investigations started during the period March 31st to May 12th, 1967. The birds caught were identified, sexed and weighed. They were then

55

closely examined for any possible seeds or other organisms, which might be attached to the exterior of the body; thereafter the birds were dissected and their alimentary tract cleaned of content. If there were seeds present, they were identified and tested for germination. Finally, the grit from the gizzard was inspected, as minerals or rock types so found might reveal where the last intake of food occurred.

Of the total number of 97 birds of 14 different species, none of the birds carried seed on their exterior. A few birds carried nematodes and other parasites. Of the total birds caught, 32 were snow buntings of the nominate race, *Plectrophenaz nivalis nivalis*, which is not native to Iceland but migrates via Iceland to Greenland from the British Isles and differs from the Icelandic race. Of these, 10 individuals had seeds in addition to grit in their gizzards. The 10 birds carried with them 87 seeds, the majority of which seemed viable. Plants from two seeds were grown to maturity (*Polygonum persicaria* and *Carex bigelowii*) (Fig. 10.5).

The records indicate that only the snow buntings of the nominate race were seed carriers. That the seeds were in the gizzard and none in the stomach indicates that the birds had not been

Fig. 10.5. Polygonum persicaria grown from seed that was carried to Surtsey by a snow bunting.

caught feeding, but had apparently consumed the seeds at an earlier time. The accompanying rocks and minerals definitely show that the birds had not been on the mainland of Iceland, i.e. there was no old Icelandic basalt in the gizzards. There were in addition some grains of cinder picked up in Surtsey; but of greater importance was that rock types and foreign sediments, which must have been collected by the birds outside Iceland, were found in the gizzards.

Most of the seeds identified from the gizzards were of species rather common both in Iceland and the British Isles, such as crowberry, *Empetrum*, a club-rush, *Scirpus*, and a spurry, *Spergula*, as well as the common black sedge, *Carex nigra*, and also *Polygonum persicaria*, a European species, which only survives in Iceland near cultivated areas and warm springs.

One seed was identified as bog-rosemary, *Andromeda polifolia*. This plant is definitely not found growing in Iceland, but is native to Greenland as well as the British Isles, where it is found in bogs from Somerset to the Hebrides. A few seeds are with hesitation identified as those of alfalfa, *Medicago sativa*. If this is correct, it would almost eliminate both Greenland and Iceland from being the place of origin of the seeds. The conclusion is, that the seed in the gizzards of the snow buntings, together with the mineral grit, were picked up by the birds in the British Isles and carried by them over the ocean to Surtsey on their migration to Greenland via Iceland. That the seeds were picked up in Surtsey with the Surtsey ash is doubtful. Should the former statement be true, it would prove that birds transport seed over long distances and some seeds retain viability.

In 1968 the capture of migrating birds was repeated. Three assistants stayed on the island during the period April 16th to May 10th and collected over 200 birds of various species. The birds were dissected and their alimentary tracts cleaned of content. This content was then inspected for organisms; when seeds were present, they were classified and tested for germination. The grit from the gizzard was inspected for minerals, which might reveal its origin and thus the possible location of the last food intake. Of the 200 birds caught, only five were snow buntings of the same nominate race. Four of these birds were found to carry seeds in their alimentary tract. As in previous years, the seeds were found in the gizzard. No other birds carried seeds.

From these birds ten seeds of two species were obtained. Six were identified as seed of *Silene* species, possibly of campion *S. uniflora*, which is common in Iceland. Four seeds were, however, those of *Carex nigra* (*C. fusca* All., *C. goodenowii* Gay.), which is a sedge common to Iceland. When tested for viability, one of the *Carex* seeds germinated and grew to the seedling stage. Seed of this same species was also found in the snow buntings caught on Surtsey in 1967.

These observations on Surtsey demonstrate that snow buntings of all migratory birds are most likely to be carriers of seeds. It also shows that the seeds of various plants can reach the island by dispersal and that both *Polygonum persicaria* and the *Carex* seeds at least retain their germination ability following such a transport over the ocean.

Effects of the Transport

Ever since Surtsey was created various living beings have landed on the island. The majority of these have been migrants and visitors that have come by chance having little means to settle in this harsh habitat of the island. These organisms have been carried from the neighboring areas that are fertile and rich in plant and animal life. These areas differ in size and distances from Surtsey, but in addition vary in vegetation and fauna. It is thus obvious that the individual locations have different opportunity to influence life on Surtsey.

Of all the vascular plant species found in Surtsey as living individuals or diaspores it is estimated that 80% have come from the neighboring islands or Heimaey. Around 17% may have come from the mainland and only 3% of seeds discovered may have been carried over longer distances (Fig. 10.6).

A special transport character of the organism obviously influences greatly the dispersal opportunity of the species. Plants with seeds that can float or are light as well as spores that are easily carried by wind or water have a better chance than others to get to Surtsey. Similarly some animals are more mobile and hardier in comparison to others and are thus more capable colonizers.

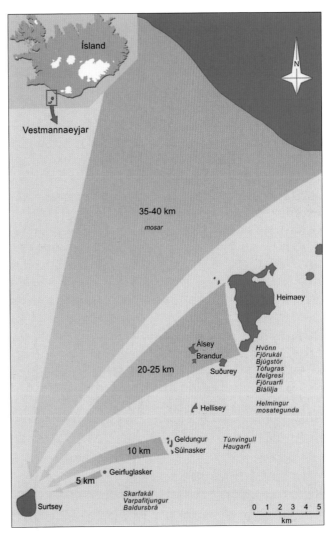

Fig. 10.6. A map showing a possible dispersal of diaspores from nearby sources.

Most of the vascular plants that at present are found growing on Surtsey, have been brought as seed or fruit with birds from the nearby islands. More rarely seeds have been picked up by birds on the mainland of Iceland or still farther away and carried to the island (Fig. 10.6). Approximately 75% of the vascular plant species found on Surtsey today have been carried to the island by birds.

The first vascular plants transported to Surtsey were almost exclusively coastal species obviously carried by ocean currents or brought in by birds from the neighboring shores. Surtsey being an island with a sandy foreshore and the neighboring land masses having a highly maritime vegetation increase the possibility of dispersal of such coastal plants, whereas plants from

57

sources farther away have less chance of dispersal. It may be estimated that 20% of the vascular plants on Surtsey have dispersed by sea to the island. Air currents have carried only a small number or 5% of the vascular plants.

As far as animals are concerned, the lower organisms of the smallest size and greatest tolerance of unfavorable environments have shown the greatest ability for a successful transport. Flying insects and arachnids have also proven quite capable of air dispersal to Surtsey, whereas soil animals and land mammals have had little or no chance of dispersal to the island. Lately, however, earth-worms have been discovered in Surtsey. Birds have an easy access to Surtsey, whereas other vertebrates of the Icelandic fauna have not reached the island, except seals, that come and breed there annually on the beaches. The dispersal of marine animals is a different matter compared to the terrestrial organisms. The ocean is their natural way of transport.

Organisms Recorded

Thanks to the thorough observations on Surtsey and the detailed recordings of biological events, which were started shortly after the island was formed and have continued ever since, it has been possible to study closely the colonization by various organisms, and to follow the numerous attempts of establishment with all its failures and sometime successes.

In the following chapters an account will be given of the first attempts of individuals to colonize the island. These included both higher and lower forms of life; plants and animals, that are common in the ocean around the Westman Islands and on the islands of the archipelago. The invasion of these organisms has taken place both on the socle of the island, as well as on the dry land of Surtsey, with the result that parts of the volcanic cone are now spotted with vegetation and various colonies of animals.

In order to facilitate a better orientation during various investigations on the island, a team of surveyors proceeded in 1967 to fix a co-ordinate system onto a map of Surtsey and to select quadrats representing four typical substrates. For this purpose, certain points were established throughout the island. These were later identified with conspicuous marks for aerial photography. The Surtsey map was in that way connected with the Icelandic co-ordinate system. Squares, each one hectare in area, were then drawn on the map and identified by a letter and a number like squares on a checkerboard, e. g. A1 B2. This co-ordinate system was then used extensively as an aid in locating the various sites of study on the island (Fig. 10.7). To start with every individual colonist was marked with a stake. Later different ecological methods have been applied for measuring individuals and communities as well as distribution of species.

Since 1990 some 22 permanent plots 10x10 m in area have been set up for studying the development of vegetation and soil in the various habitats on the island. And at the same time GPS instruments have been used to record locations of rare individuals observed on Surtsey.

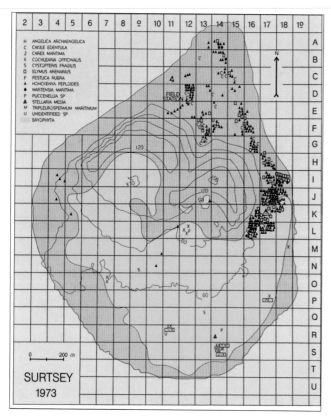

Fig. 10.7. Distribution maps of Surtsey with quadrat mesh were used for registering events.

11. Marine research

During the volcanic eruption the cinder cone built up from a depth of 130 m and covered an area of 6.5 sq. km, of which 2.8 sq. km were above water. The smaller satellite volcanoes added each approximately 1 sq. km to the submarine base of the Surtsey structure. This cinder pile with the lava crust, which during the latter part of the volcanic activity flowed down its southern side, covered and destroyed all the benthic organisms of a part of the sea floor. At the edges of the submarine cone the layer of ash gradually thinned out and its effect dwindled. The ash, however, reached as far out as one nautical mile off the island, where a thin layer of ash was measured over a layer of mud. This had somewhat affected the benthic life, and fewer animals were obtained there during dredging in April 1964 than sampled at a station farther away.

The phyto- and zoo-plankton around the island, however, had not been affected. This was demonstrated by numerous samples taken from the ocean around the island during special surveys in the months following the beginning of the eruption, and with the aid of the continuous plankton recorder of the M/S Gullfoss that passed Surtsey every third week during the first winter and every other week during the summer.

The mechanical activities of the tephra, pressure during explosions and high temperatures, undoubtedly influenced locally the pelagic life at the site of eruption, though the effects were minimal some metres out.

During the first oceanographic survey in the area that took place on November 15th to 16th 1963, no increase in sea temperature was, for example, noticed at a 300 m distance from the eruption centre, and various surveys that followed revealed the same findings. This was especially noticeable during the period of tephra formation. When lava started to flow into the sea there was, however, some rise in temperature. In July 1964 a temperature of 30 to 40 °C was once recorded at 50 m distance from the edge of the lava. But in general, the effect of the eruption upon the sea-water was negligible. The salinity was not changed and there was only a slight increase in some nutrients, which may have been due to greater turbulence near the island and a reduced biological uptake by organisms that now had disappeared.

Marine Algae

Marine algae were among the first plants to drift to Surtsey. Knotted wrack *Ascophyllum nodosum* was occasionally washed ashore during the first summer of the island's existence, and a few pieces of thallus from *Fucus distichus* and *Fucus vesiculosus* were recorded as well on the beach in 1964. But during that first year no macroscopic benthic algae had yet attached to the recently developed, naked substrate. Lava was still flowing towards the south, but on the northeastern part of the island the edge of the lava flow was already broken up into boulders, which had rolled towards the sand on the northern ness. On this 'older' lava, which at that time was four to five months old, microscopic organisms were getting settled. There were some marine bacteria, and diatoms, which on closer study were identified as *Navicula mollis* and *Nitzschia bilobata*. These were pioneers of the marine benthic vegetation of Surtsey.

In the summer of 1965 some filamentous green algae had been added to the marine flora of the island. These algae, which proved to be

Urospora penicilliformis, grew as isolated tufts in pure population at the high-tide level on a lava cliff at the western side of Surtsey. The sandy beach to the north, on the other hand, seemed to be an unsuitable habitat for the benthic biota, nor did dredging on the lava sea floor at 15 to 20 m depth south of the island show any signs of life.

The rather slow process of colonization of the marine algae on Surtsey may be considered to be due to the relative isolation of the island and the severe environmental conditions. The substrate of Surtsey as such was perfectly suitable for colonization. This could be demonstrated by transferring stones from Surtsey, placing them in a well-established floral surrounding and observing how organisms would get attached. The rocks were colonized by eight species of algae within one and a half months. But the dispersal to Surtsey takes a longer time, although there is luxuriant marine vegetation on the adjacent islands, the nearest of which is Geirfuglasker 5.5 km away, which has about 100 species of algae excluding diatoms.

The various marine algae that have washed ashore as driftweed, show that macroscopic fragments can serve as diaspores, but the microscopic spores are also being dispersed by means of sea currents. All the species reaching Surtsey, obviously, do not necessarily colonize its coast.

On the other hand, selective immigration gradually started to take place on the virgin substrate of Surtsey. Thus in the summer of 1966, the rate of colonization increased markedly and a noticeable zonation was formed in the supra-littoral and eu-littoral regions with three distinct communities. A green belt, 0.50 to 8.30 m wide, of vigorously growing *Urospora penicilliformis* occupied the rocks by the southern lava apron and the boulders on the east coast. The species grew mostly in a pure stand, but in some places the associated species were *Ulothrix flacca*, *Ulothrix pseudoflacca* and *Enteromorpha flexuosa*. Immediately below this belt the species *Porphyra umbilicalis* had established a colony. This was not surprising, as these species are also represented in the algal communities of the adjacent coasts.

Distinct from the green belt and below it, extending down to the lowest part of the intertidal region, was a zone of brown filamentous diatoms, mainly, composed of *Navicula mollis* forming a dense slippery coating on the rocks. And among these were some young plants of the kelp *Alaria esculenta*. It was interesting to note that the pioneer species of this region were again the filamentous benthic diatoms. It is likely that the first step in the algal succession of similar areas is always a seral stage of diatoms. The second step is the colonization of *Urospora mirabilis* at the high-water mark of the intertidal region and *Alaria esculenta* at the lower water mark (Fig. 11.1).

The third community had established itself in the tide-pools of the upper littoral region, where *Petalonia zosterifolia* was the dominant species associated with scattered individuals of such species as *Pylaiella littoralis*, *Ectocarpus confervoides* and *Petalonia fascia*, to be joined in the following year by the species *Acrosiphonia arcta*.

In 1967 there were altogether 14 species of benthic algae discovered growing on Surtsey, excluding diatoms, and in 1968 this figure had increased to 27 species.

In the upper part of the littoral fringe *Urospora*

Fig. 11.1. Seaweed on the pedestal of Surtsey. Kelp, Alaria esculenta *(light yellow) and laver* Porphyra umbilicalis.

penicilliformis was now found everywhere associated with *Ulothrix* species, and below it on the northwest coast was a belt with *Petalonia fascia* and *P. zosterifolia*, which are subsided by *Porphyra umbilicalis* and *Enteromorpha* species. The upper limit of this belt is at about 1.30 m above low-water mark.

Below this, at the lowest part of the littoral region, was the bare belt which, in some places, was occupied by diatoms. In the sub-littoral region *Alaria esculenta* dominated with a cover of up to 80 individuals per sq. m at 12 m depth. Below 10 m depth the *Alaria* was often associated with *Desmarestia* species and *Monostroma grevillei*.

At deep-water below 20 m there was a scattered vegetation of red algae such as *Porphyra miniata*, *Antithamnionella floccosa*, *Phycodrys rubens* and *Polysiphonia stricta*. The growth of these recent invaders was on a stable substrate. No growth had occupied the unstable sand of the northern site.

In 1970 the marine vegetation at Surtsey had increased to 35 species of algae and 11 of diatoms. This rapid increase of species was not so much at the beach, as the substrate there is still unstable. On the other hand, the increase was more at greater depths under the tidal-zone, where there was less movement of water and the stable substrate of rocks gave the algae a firmer support. These species were apparently all primary colonists and later invaders had not yet arrived.

During the year 1977 the first *Rhodophysema elegans* arrived. It was found south of the island at 10 m depth. By then several species of red algae were beginning to settle at greater depths, such as *Lomentaria clavellosa* and *Plocamium cartilagineum*. After some thirty years there were 53 species of larger types of algae found at Surtsey, which is about half the number of species known from the Westman Island area. Of these 22 were found in the intertidal zone, whereas 31 were growing at greater depths.

In 1997 altogether 76 species had been recorded, omitting diatoms. The most noteworthy of the new species was to find two young specimens of spiral wrack *Fucus spiralis* in the upper part of the littoral zone on a rock at the eastern shore.

The marine vegetation on Surtsey has apparently not yet reached the climax community. The

Fig. 11.2. Barnacles and goose barnacles on a float found drifted up on the beach of Surtsey.

kelp forests are still thin compared to those of the older islands. The greatest cover was, however, measured 89.5% at 30 m.

Many of the most common species of the adjacent areas have now colonized on the socle of Surtsey. The new colonizers are mostly found in the archipelago of the Westman Island except for the species *Porphyra purpurea*, which is new to Icelandic waters. It was also unexpected to find *Omphalophyllum ulvaceum* in Surtsey at 10 m depht as the species has not previously been found in southern Iceland.

Marine Fauna

It has previously been stressed that the volcanic eruption had little effect on the pelagic biota of the ocean around the island. These waters are relatively rich in marine life, and as a matter of fact the banks around the Westman Islands are some of the best fishing grounds in Iceland. During the eruption the fishing continued around Surtsey, and the catch was no less than in the years before.

When walking on the shores of Surtsey, one was repeatedly reminded of the presence of the luxuriant marine animal life. A school of small dab could be seen swimming in the tidal water, and occasionally a few individuals would strand in the sand or be washed ashore. On other occasions a number of lumpfish young would get into the tide-pools and strand, or a red squid might be washed upon the black basaltic sand. Sometimes the shores were literally swarming with euphausids left there by the receding tide.

On driftwood and floats from nets that had been washed up on the beach one could observe colonies of goose barnacles *Lepas* spp. that were settling on material foreign to the Surtsey shores, while the primary virgin substrate of the island was not colonized by acorn barnacles *Balanus balanoides,* until several years later (Fig 11.2).

In December 1963 plankton samples were collected on a transect from one to twelve nautical miles west of the island and again in January 1964, which showed that pelagic animal life was normal and had apparently not been affected by the eruption. During a trawling survey in December 1963, five and a half nautical miles west of Surtsey, the catch consisted of eight species of fish as well as Norway lobster. This was further proof that life was normal in the Surtsey waters.

However, the benthic animals had been destroyed, but while the island was still under formation, the colonization of the benthic animals started, and the sediment of sand, sunken pumice and scoria were gradually being invaded by numerous pelagic larvae. The dispersal of these larvae is largely dependent on the distance they have to travel to a new substrate from the potential parent population. The longer the distance, the less the chances that the current will bring the larvae to the new habitat.

Already in November of 1964 eight animals were taken by a scraper from a depth of 70 m at 0.2 nautical miles west of the island. Two of these animals were the tube-dwelling trumpet worm *Pectinaria koreni*. The bottom there was rough scoria, and this same substrate reached out to 0.4 nautical miles from the shore, except to the north where the side is mostly gravel. Farther out the bottom was more covered with the finer volcanic material. There the ash had not seemingly affected the fauna. Still farther out the ash was so thin that it was ineffective,

In 1966 some bottom samples were collected at 100 m depth. The species found indicated the presence of the most common animals, such as 17 species of marine bristle worms, polychaeta. On the slope in shallower water, the trumpet worm also occurred with other polychaetes such as *Scoloplos armiger* and *Capitella capitata.*

There were also found six bivalve species of which the most common was the glossy furrow-shell *Abra nitida*, and some brittle stars, which were represented by the species *Ophiura affinis*.

It was noted that the polychaets species were the first animals to invade the rather barren lava. Although they are known to feed on organic contents of the sediment they were also making use of particles suspended in the water. The latter food source was undoubtedly more abundant at that time. The settlement of these and other animals on the slopes was, however, repeatedly destroyed by deposits of tephra produced by the volcanic islands of Syrtlingur and Jólnir and by later eruptions of lava on Surtsey.

In 1967 most of the life on the slope had been killed off. But on the lower levels it had evidently not been affected and seemed to be fairly normal. From there these animals could once more crawl on the newly formed substrate up the base of the pedestal on Surtsey.

Some of this unstable tephra, on the contrary, was to the benefit of marine animals. The pumice produced during the eruption floated on the ocean surface and drifted back and forth over long distances until it was washed upon a far away shore or sank to the ocean floor.

During this drifting of the pumice great quantities of the particles served as floats for goose barnacles. The larvae of these animals, which every year swarm the ocean in enormous numbers, suddenly found an unusual opportunity of attachment and means of transport, especially following the pumice production from Syrtlingur in 1965. A cargo of millions of goose barnacles was thus transported towards the Reykjanes peninsula where the load was deposited on the southern shores, or where it became, suddenly, an important item in the diet of the Icelandic sea-gulls. As a matter of fact, this incident was first noticed in the course of an investigation of the feeding habits of sea-gulls, when quite unexpectedly, in the autumn of 1965, up to 70% of their diet consisted of goose barnacles. When an explanation was sought, the shores were found to be covered with pumice carrying barnacles belonging to three species:

Dosima fascicularis, Lepas anatifera *and* L. pectinata. *The last named species had not previously been recorded in Iceland. Thus the effects of an eruption can even aid in the dispersal of certain species.*

In the following years the sediment on the slopes of Surtsey gradually became more stable and was, in deep water, invaded by the same species as well as new ones of the infauna, and gradually, the communities on Surtsey are reaching the same balance as those of the adjacent islands.

Higher up the pedestal of Surtsey in shallower water, the fauna had some difficulties in colonizing due to the continuous fall of ash and flow of lava. The substrate was thus very unstable, and the scouring effect of sharp tephra particles was hard on the juvenile colonists. It was not until early summer of 1967 that the first acorn barnacle *Balanus balanoides* was discovered in a sheltered hollow of the lower part of the littoral region.

Gradually a colony of acorn barnacles formed a zone in- between the littoral fringe and the eulittoral region on the boulders and the cliffs of the southern lava apron of the island.

In 1967 SCUBA-divers found hydroids on the rocks at 20 m depth. At the same time species of nematodes were discovered, these were crawling in the ground layer where they may have been feeding on some decaying algae. There they also found colonies of moss animals, Bryozoa, of which the sea mat *Membranipora membranacea* was most common in the inter-tidal zone.

Four species of bivalves *Lamellibranchia* with pelagic larvae were discovered in the autumn of 1967 in the inter-tidal as well as the sub-littoral region. The most abundant of these were the saddle oyster *Heteranomia squamula* and the common mussel *Mytilus edulis*.

In the sublittoral region the pioneers of decapoda were the shrimp *Eualus pusiolus*, the spider crab *Hyas coarctatus* and the blue crab *Portunus holsatus*, and in that same year a few species of copepods and sand hoppers, amphipods, were also recorded. In addition to this, the SCUBA-divers observed a number of crabs on the rocky bottom down to 20 m depth.

In the following years the tidal region was fur-

ther colonized by the acorn barnacle and the common mussel. These two species obviously predominate in the tidal zone and the region in which the mussel had colonized, extending down to some 30 m in the sub-tidal region. At these sites the soft coral of the species "dead men's fingers" *Alcyonium digitatum* were first observed in 1969. These animals have later spread out on the pedestal at this depth.

In 1974 there had been an addition of seven new species of marine animals on the socle of Surtsey. Among these were brittle stars, the common whelk *Buccinum undatum* and the isopod *Idothea granulosa* that were seen there for the first time. Then in 1980 there was still an addition of new colonists as eleven new species were identified. Among these were both sea-gherkins *Cucumaria frondosa* and sea-urchins *Echinoidea*. During the following years there were not many new intro-

Fig. 11.3. On this photograph, taken in deep waters, a starfish is seen feeding on mussels that have now established on the pedestal of Surtsey.

Fig. 11.4. Hydrozoan on the socle of Surtsey at 30 m depth.

63

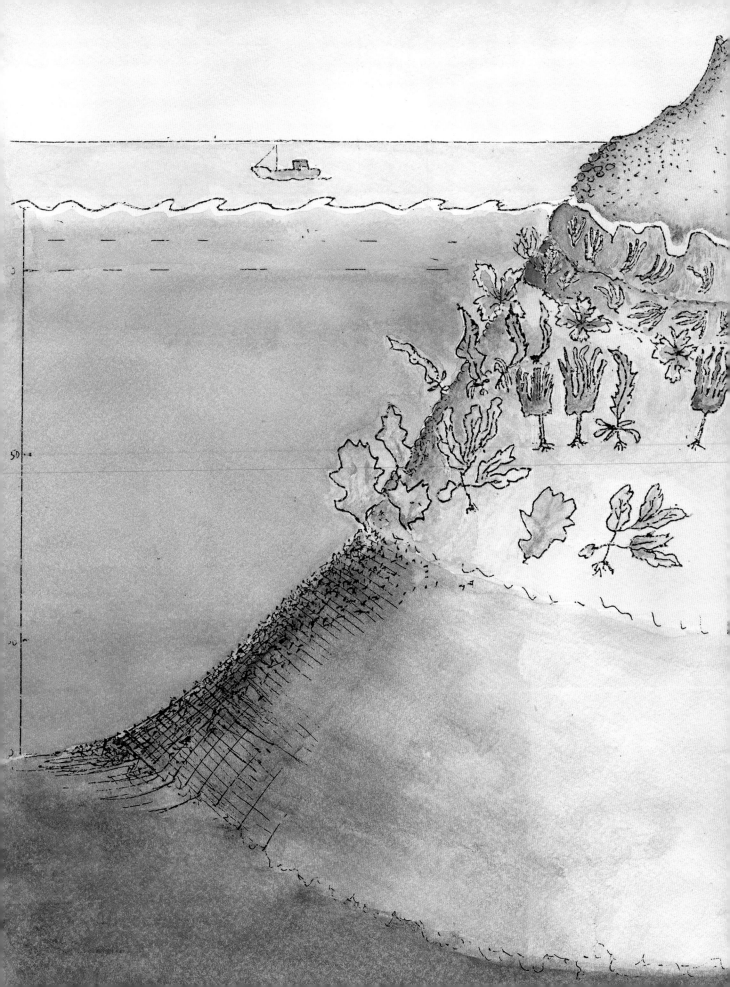

ductions until 1987 when 28 species of marine animals were recorded. In this new group were seven species of bivalves. It was the first time that the scallop *Chlamys islandicus* was observed.

In 1992 samples were collected on three transects from the subtidal zone where some 78 species of benthic animals could be identified at the eastern coast of Surtsey, but only 40 species were found at the west coast. On the southern coast most of the species were found at 30 m depht. No new species were found in 1997 when the benthic coastal fauna was once more investigated on the same three transects. Most of the species at that time had a wide depht-distribution

The species of marine animals having been recorded are not necessarily found on the socle every year. This may be due to chance, as when the SCUBA- diver overlooks the species at the time of diving, but the reason could also be because the newcomers are not evenly fit to colonize the new habitat. Some have had to abandon the place and yield the ground for others better fit in the competition for survival (Fig.11.3 and 11.4).

However, the coast all around Surtsey is a very unstable habitat for the marine animals due to the swell and heavy beating of the Atlantic Ocean.

A comparative study of the benthic fauna of adjacent islands shows that the most common species, in these areas, are gradually colonizing the recently formed substrate of Surtsey. At present all the most common animals of this area are now also found at Surtsey. It is becoming rare to find a new species at the island.

Furthermore, the vertical distribution of species found in the numerous samplings so far performed indicates that the classical zonation occurring elsewhere in these areas is also taking place on Surtsey. The most mobile species with pelagic larvae and those that are abundant in the adjacent regions were the first to settle on the pedestal. Some of these species are also known to be especially tolerant to environmental changes, such as variations in temperature, salinity, depth and texture of the substrate. They were thus well equipped to become pioneers on Surtsey. Later arrivals were individuals of less frequent or rare species.

Fig. 11.5. Marine organism on the pedestal of Surtsey. Algae to left. Animals to right.

Because of the very intensive study on Surtsey, it has been possible even to discover species that are new to the Westman Islands, such as the barnacle *Balanus hammeri*, the amphipod *Calliopius laeviusculus* and the sea squirt *Ascidia callosa* that were discovered in 1968 and which, as a matter of fact, are new to the south coast of Iceland. Three species of amphipods found on Surtsey in 1992-97 are also new to the Icelandic fauna.

As the vegetation increases on the pedestal of Surtsey the marine animals that live on it become more luxuriant and form numerous food chains. On the seaweed live hydrozoans and sea mats. Up on the rocks and boulders of the tidal zone colonies of the common mussels have settled, and on these in turn sit barnacles and other sessile animals.

In this new association live both parasites and scavengers. The common starfish *Asterias rubens* comes to look for and enjoy eating the mussel and the banded chink-shell crawls on the brown kelp blades to live on the small sessile animals that in turn feed on the marine vegetation. In the young kelp-forest various fishes swim, searching for food. There the short-spined sea scorpions frequent as well as lumpsuckers and sea snails *Liparis* seeking the smaller animals that are living in the algal-vegetation. Thus an ecosystem is gradually being formed on the pedestal of Surtsey, with the interaction between many of the individuals, that are known from other associations of marine organisms around the coast of Iceland. (Fig 11.5)

Higher up in the food chain of animals that so far have occupied the waters around Surtsey and are forming communities in this newly developed habitat, there exist various species of large and small fish. Thus the capelin *Mallotus villosus* passes Surtsey in enormous quantities and is in turn consumed by cod *Gadus morrhua*, haddock *Melanogrammus aeglefinus* and saithe *Polachius virens*.

The shores of Surtsey are also frequently visited by seals. The seals lie there and rest and are not met with any disturbance. Since 1983 both Common and Grey seals have annually bred on the island. They find this region abundant in food, as do the ocean birds and fishermen from the Westman Islands.

12. Terrestrial research

Bacteria and Moulds

From the records of diaspores washed upon the shores of Surtsey it may be inferred that there already existed an organic source of energy on the island for various living organisms. The most effective contributors of such organic matter were the thousands of sea-gulls that roost on the island and constantly fly around its shores. Some of the edges of the tephra hills were already in the first summer white with bird excrement. Another major energy source was a variety of debris washed up by the sea. This was mostly confined to the beach, especially to the high-tide level, or a belt marked by the average tidal amplitude of 2.5 m. On the northern ness this belt has become increasingly broad. The ness may be completely inundated during high spring tides and is therefore littered with debris.

This organic matter carried to the island is mainly in the form of seaweed and kelp, all sorts of driftwood, logs, tree stumps, boards, and also varieties of carcasses of birds, fish and other marine animals. To this may be added strings and pieces of nets and all sorts of trash discarded from fishing-boats in the surrounding waters. All this material is a secondary source of energy in the ecosystem of Surtsey, which may be used by some of the local organisms and will influence in a number of ways the development of life on the island.

During the summer of 1964 it could be noted that fragments of seaweed and carcasses were decaying at the high-tide mark and were obviously being utilized by bacteria. These processes of breakdown were however not of special interest, and the micro-organisms attacking these organic items would not differ markedly from those found elsewhere on any southern shore of Iceland.

The drifting of debris to the island continues, but there is no marked increase in organic deposit from one year to another. Some of the debris is undoubtedly buried in the sand, other is washed out again, and the carcasses on the shore are immediately cleaned up by the numerous sea-gulls that constantly search the shore for any kind of food.

The primary source of energy in the Surtsey ecosystem is sunlight, which can be utilized by the photosynthetic plants that are gradually colonizing the island, though no such plants were presant during the first years of the island's existence.

On Surtsey energy was also available as thermal energy from the volcanic activity or the energy produced by chemical reactions. Through the catalysis of such energy some simple organic compounds of abiogenic origin might even have been formed. This primary energy source available for the earliest micro-organisms of the Surtsey ecosystem was of major interest for the study of the first steps in a biological succession, starting with the colonization of primitive micro-organisms on the inert substrate, and ending with a highly developed climax community containing numerous lower and higher organisms.

Although the shores of Surtsey soon obtained scattered deposits of organic matter of foreign origin, the main part of the island was clean and devoid of these materials, and literally speaking completely sterile at the time of the formation of the island. The substrate was even repeatedly sterilized by the rain of volcanic ash from the eruption of the smaller islands that spread many layers of tephra over most of its original surface. But even a desolated island does not remain free of micro-organisms for any length of time. Small organisms soon settle on such islands.

The microflora invading Surtsey mainly dispersed by ocean and by air. During stormy weather the waves may splash sea foam far upon the island and bring with it various marine micro-organisms. There they will encounter a new environment both regarding salinity and pH. The latter has been found to vary in the top layer of tephra in the range from pH 4.2 to 6.5. Some of marine micro-organisms were capable of establishing themselves on the Surtsey substrate, especially in the ocean beach interface. When substrate from the beach was investigated, a number of bacteria and moulds were obtained.

The airborne microflora was measured on Surtsey on various occasions, and the quantity of organisms in the air was compared with that above cultivated and populated areas. These tests proved that there was a constant microbial dispersal by the air currents to the island, but the microflora of the air over Surtsey was scanty in species and low in number of individuals per volume compared with counts in the air of highly developed communities on the adjacent island of Heimaey and on the mainland of Iceland (Figure 12.1). It was noted that direction and velocity of wind affected the quantity of airborne organisms. During northerly winds, soil dust was brought from the mainland, and at the same time the air carried an increased number of organisms to the island, but living conditions were difficult.

Despite the precipitation in the Surtsey area being quite high, no rainwater accumulates in any amount on the island; it seeps right through the porous substrates, whether it is of lava, tephra or sand. During droughts, the surface consequently does not hold sufficient moisture to support the life of micro-organisms. Where moisture is present, however, both algal and bacterial life has been able to establish itself. Many fumaroles that are still active provide, for example, moisture that condenses in surrounding crevasses. Microscopic examinations of such habitats have revealed a few bacteria per sample. Roots and rhizoids of plants growing on Surtsey all had a high bacterial population. Such bacteria may have been brought to the island attached to the diaspores and are now growing on the organic material excreted by the higher plants.

Some of the habitats on Surtsey are quite unique in respect to diversity and extremes in temperature, such as the fumaroles and the hot areas, which have various gradients of temperature and moisture. There the bacteri-

Fig. 12.1. Petri-dishes were set up for trapping airborne organisms.

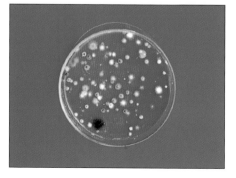

ologists have observed in small numbers both Thiobacillus thiooxidans and T. ferrooxidans, whereas denitrifying and nitrifying bacteria were more frequent. In 1976 the species Azotobacter was discovered, but that species lives symbiotically with higher plants and is known for it's nitrifying activities. The moulds, which are found on roots of higher plants, were very likely brought with the diaspores to the island, but mould spores are apparently also dispersing to Surtsey. Moulds have been found on carcasses and bird droppings and can be considered common on decaying organic material on the island. Spores of various other fungi are easily carried to the island, where they can start developing if they have suitable media to grow on. Mushrooms have been found in Surtsey since 1975, mostly two species of the genus Omphalina. One of them grows in symbiosis with algae and forms a kind of lichen that grows on the lava among the moss. The other is Omphalina rustica, which needs organic compounds for its development. Lately there has been a great increase of mushrooms in the bird colony on the southern parts of the lava, on soil, which is being enriched by the bird droppings (Fig. 12.2).

Algae

The marine algae were pioneer colonizers of Surtsey's pedestal, and became abundant in the littoral region a few years after the formation of the island. In contrast to this the dryland algae of Surtsey have in general not been so conspicuous in the terrestrial ecosystem. It has often been suggested that algae are the pioneer plants on new substrata. This idea is partly based on the discoveries on the volcanic island of Krakatoa, Indonesia, where blue-green algae were found to be early colonizers. This, however, has not been the case on Surtsey, and the algal mats, which are now found in a few places on the island, are mostly formed by the coccoid green algae.

Marine algae apparently disperse in great quantities by ocean and can colonize the new substrate within a short time. In contrast, the terrestrial algae do not withstand much salinity, and their dispersal to Surtsey mostly takes place by wind via the air. It has also been demonstrated on Surtsey that birds carry algal spores and tissues on their feet, and it had even been suggested that insects play a minor part in dispersal of algae.

The transport of terrestrial algae is, however, more restricted than is the dispersal of marine algae via the ocean route. Thus air transport, for example, seems to be selective towards species with small size organisms. This difference in means of dispersal and therefore also in the quantity of capable colonizers is, however, not a sufficient cause to explain the slow rate of colonization of the terrestrial algae on the dryland of Surtsey, compared with the rapid development of societies of marine algae on the socle of the island. The variation in the algae population in these two biomes is rather due to a difference in their environmental conditions. Thus, the substratum below sea-level mainly serves as a mechanical support for the organisms, the nutritive matter being available in the salt water, while the terrestrial algae are dependent on nutrition from the dryland substratum. Similarly, the toxic effect of the volcanic salts has been readily washed out of the substrata below sea-level, but may be detrimental to algae in the dryland biome. The erosive effect of the tephra blown back and forth by the wind may be more harmful than similar abrasive effect of tephra, which is washed by the waves. The greatest difference in the environment of these two biomes, however, remains in the availability of water. In the terrestrial habitats the substrate, whether it is the solid lava or the loose tephra, is often

Fig. 12.2. *The mushroom* Omphalina rustica *grows on a fertile substrate in the bird colony on the southern side of the lava field.*

low in moisture. This periodical lack of water in the superficial substrata of the dryland is apparently the greatest hindrance to the algal establishment, while there is obviously no such water shortage below sea-level.

While various algae are thus rather readily dispersed to Surtsey, they are in general not able to establish or to become dominant plants in the dryland communities.

Compared with the numerous bacteria, which have been recorded in the air or on the cinder surface, a smaller variety of blue-green algae have been collected on Surtsey and isolated by enrichment culture techniques. The accumulation of these airborne algae is apparently most abundant at the base of the cinder cones, as they may be washed down with rain and carried to lower levels with the run-off water. Thus the greatest amount of blue-green algal species have been recorded at the base of the southern slope of the tephra cones.

Fig. 12.3. Stereocoulon vesuvianum *is a lichen growing on lava near the Surtungur crater.*

Some stable algal settlements, however, exist on Surtsey, and in a few places, layers of algae may be observed. Some algae have been able to establish themselves where moisture levels are high in crevices of lava, or where steam condenses from fumaroles. On the edges of some such fumaroles the ash particles gradually stabilize, forming a compact, moist crust on which colonies of algae could establish.

In 1968 eight species of blue-green algae were recorded in the area of the two central craters, as well as 100 other algal species including 74 diatoms. These were either discovered together or in association with bacteria and mosses, the largest colony being 30 sq. cm in area.

The development continued in the following years, and the number of species in the small oasis around the fumaroles increased. These algal settlements, however, have not become conspicuous, and the blue-green algae are quite unimportant as primary colonizers of Surtsey. One exception to this was a wet spot around a bucket filled with rain-water placed on the lava as a trap to attract birds. In this artificial habitat, which received a large amount of bird droppings, a mat of blue-green algae had been formed in 1972, occupied by *Oscillatoria.*

Following the increasing size of the bird breeding colonies there have been formed ideal conditions for algal growth by the birds nests, were fertilizer is in abundance.

The primary colonizers, on Surtsey, however, did not all have a chance to rely on organic supply of nitrogen from other organisms. Some algae do not need such assistance, since they can fix their own nitrogen from the air. Such is the species *Anabaena variabilis* of blue-green algae first discovered on the island in 1968. The following year three *Nostoc* species were also among the algae recorded. These species have the ability of fixing molecular nitrogen and could participate in the lichen formation. The nitrogen fixation is, however, rather slow under the Surtsey conditions compared with warmer habitats, and cannot be considered of major ecological importance in the development of vascular plants and animals on Surtsey.

The algal species represented in the microflora of Surtsey are largely identical to the flora of Icelandic soils. The colonists on Surtsey, however, seem to be of species that are of rather small size or are easily transported by spore forms. Although the algae are not necessarily pioneers in the substrate, they are often found in close relationship with the first colonizers of higher plants and are generally represented at the locations occupied by moss.

In the high-temperature areas surrounding steam vents near the old Surtur crater, some of the blue-green algae form a faint green colour. This area is occupied by the thermophilic species *Mastigocladus laminosus* that grows at temperatures in the range between 57 to 64 °C and in hot springs of alkaline to neutral pH. This thermophilic species is a cosmopolitan blue-green alga, which is common in the hot springs on the mainland of Iceland, those closest to Surtsey being at a distance of 75 km. The inoculum, which was transported to Surtsey, may have dispersed by air or by birds from these sources. But if precautions are not taken, scientists working in thermal areas may also become agents of dispersal.

Lichens

It is a widely held belief that lichens are pioneer forms of life in the colonization of new rocky substrata. This is the case with respect to many new lava flows throughout the Icelandic mainland, especially those occurring at high altitudes. It was thus expected that lichen would be an early colonizer of the Surtsey lava. The substrate was therefore thoroughly studied every year following the formation of the island, and birds' feet were investigated to see if they could serve as means of transport for possible lichen colonists.

Surprisingly, it was not until the summer of 1970 that the first lichen was found on Surtsey. At that time two communities of lichen were, however, observed in the vicinity of the Surtungur crater. At both sites the habitats received moisture and warm air from a thermal area. One of these habitats was on a lava crust north-east of the crater. It was occupied by small specimens of *Stereocaulon vesuvianum* a common pioneer lichen on the Icelandic lava flows. The other habitat was situated on the outer side of the northern slope of the crater. This was occupied by two species, *Trapelia coarctata* and *Placopsis gelida* (Figure 12.3). This community was also better developed than the former and covered a strip of several metres in length. *T. coarctata* had not previously been recorded in Iceland, but was shortly after found on the mainland, where it was rather common in humid substrates. It is a crustose lichen so abundant on the site at Surtsey that it gave the surface of the rock a pale yellowish-brown colour.

P. gelida was represented by fewer individuals, but this is a common species on postglacial lava flows in Iceland, so it may be expected that both this species and *S. vesuvianum* will spread out in the Surtsey ecosystem. In 1971 *Stereocaulon vesuvianum* had obtained a wider distribution and was found scattered throughout the dry lava surface as well as *Stereocaulon capitellatum*. In that same year small colonies of *Acarospora* and *Bacidia* species were also noticed at the Surtungur crater.

In 1972 a bright orange-yellow patch of the species *Xanthoria candelaria* was observed near one of the plastic water tubs. It had apparently been brought there by birds since this lichen is common in Iceland where birds perch, although most of the lichen species on Surtsey must have been carried as soredia by wind to the island, as they are rather evenly distributed throughout the lava flows. Their first appearance at the Surtungur crater is only due to the favorable growth conditions there. These lichens start to develop in the minute pores on the surface of the lava.

It is noteworthy that both *Trapelia coarctata* and *Placopsis gelida* obtained a wide distribution on Surtsey and very likely they have arrived there as individual algae and mould, that later participate in the symbiotic life form of the lichen. The mould may also be able to catch *Nostock* algae, which obviously are drifting loose on the island.

It has been noted that of the three lichen species originally colonizing the lava on Surtsey, all had the nitrogen fixing blue-green algae as the third component in their symbiotic association. Very likely the blue-green algae play a major role in the colonization by the lichen of the nitrogen lacking lava. Seemingly the blue-green algae is the last one of the three to join in the symbiotic association.

In 1973 twelve lichen species had been found on Surtsey. It was noted that the lichens first occupied the newer lava. The new lava was rough and may thus have been colder than the older lava and contained more moisture. This was obvious in the autumn as the snow melted quicker off the older lava than the young one. The moist lava is most suitable for the colonization of lichen.

Mosses

It was not until the middle of August 1967 that the first moss colonies were discovered on Surtsey; these were found on a sandbank at the northern edge of the New Lagoon. The plants were all of the same species, Common Cord-moss *Funaria hygrometrica*, and in an early stage of growth. A month later, the second location of mosses was observed at the edge of the central lava crater, where the colonies consisted of two species; *Funaria hygrometrica* and Silver-moss *Bryum argenteum*.

These two moss species, the first to colonize the substrate on Surtsey, are common on the mainland of Iceland. The plants apparently grew from spores that had dispersed to the island by wind and, in the case of the communities at the lava crater, the colonization became permanent and formed a centre for further establishment of mosses on the Surtsey lava.

Fig. 12.4. A moss-cover up at the crater Surtungur.

In the following summer three new moss species were found in addition to the already existing moss population on the island. In 1969 the moss vegetation on the Surtsey lava became more conspicuous with plants occupying the lava in hollows and caverns, where sand had been deposited, and some even settling on the bare lava. The moss was, however, most vigorous where there was heat and steam emission from fumaroles, and where the vapour stabilized the sand and kept a constant moisture in the substrate.

In 1970 the number of moss species on Surtsey had increased to 16, and their distribution had extended into the southern part of the lava apron. The Common Cord-moss *F. hygrometrica* and Hoary Fringe-moss *Racomitrium canescens* were largely responsible for this distribution (Fig. 12.4). The following year several new species of moss were recorded on the island with the total distribution of 40 species gradually extending over the lava flow. The spread of growth was then mainly towards the west, but was hindered on the northern side by the tephra hills. Apparently the tephra was not a suitable habitat for any of the moss species.

Racomitrium canescens was the dominant species. However, it did not form a heavy cover, only small tufts here and there. In the years 1972 and 1973 the moss cover on Surtsey's lava developed further, but increases in distribution slowed down as compared with its rapid development in previous years, as the most favorable habitats had already been invaded.

There are large areas on the island, which have not yet been colonized by mosses. Such spots are rather hostile habitats for these plants; some too close to the splashing zone, others too sandy and erosive.

In 1973 the species of moss so far recorded on Surtsey were altogether 69, of which 64 were known to be well developed. The greatest increase of species occurred in 1972, when 32 new species were discovered, including three new species of liverworts. In the moss flora of the island only some of the species recorded are common, others are less common, rare, or very rare. The species may be grouped according to four categories, based on their abun-

dance in the various quadrats that were investigated. Thus twelve species may be considered very common, eleven species are common, seventeen were rare and twenty-four were very rare. Funaria hygrometrica, *which was one of the first moss species to arrive on Surtsey, is also one of the most abundantly and widely distributed members of the moss flora. The* Racomitrium *species arrived somewhat later, but have by now become the most dominant species on the island, especially* R. canescens, *which may also be considered one of the most common species that grow on Icelandic lava flows. The species* Bryum stenotrichum *is listed as common, but most moss species, however, are very rare on the island.*

Surtsey's original moss colonizers had to rely on dispersal of spores, which apparently derived mostly from the Icelandic mainland, by air. As the various moss species became better established, they gradually developed reproductive organs. This was studied and recorded when the species became fertile. It is worth noting that the Wooly Fringe-moss *Racomitrium lanuginosum* was found bearing capsules on Surtsey for the first time in 1972. After that the distribution of the species increased, and it became the dominant species of moss on the Surtsey lava, as it is on most Icelandic lava flows.

In our studies of the moss vegetation on Surtsey, the various habitats were recorded for each species observed in the different quadrats. The classification was based on less than five thousand observations. The records made gave the frequency of the species per quadrat as well as the favoured habitat.

The habitat classes were based on the topography of the lava, substrate, moisture and heat emission. Thus, for example, the Hoary Fringe-moss *R. canescens* was observed to be the most common species on newly formed lava flows, the habitat also favoured various other species. Another common habitat on Surtsey is the sand-covered hollow. It is favoured by many species of moss, such as various *Bryum* species and also a number of associated species, such as: Apple-moss *Philonotis*, Tread-moss *Pohlia* and Transparent Fork-moss *Dichodontium pellu-*

cidum. Other habitats are more rare and have specialised conditions. These are, for example, occupied by species that require more abundant moisture and shading conditions than the common species.

The total cover of moss on Surtsey is still rather sparse and difficult to measure due to the rough surface of the lava, however, an attempt was made to evaluate the cover of each species. The species *Bryum* (mostly Small-mouthed Tread- moss *B. stenotrichum)* and Common Cord-moss *Funaria hygrometrica* have obtained the most extensive cover, the Fringe-moss *Racomitrium* being second in coverage. The cover was greatest in the centre of the lava as well as in the Surtungur crater. Although the moss distribution started out successfully, it has slowed down lately, and at present the moss seems to be rather hard pressed in various places.

Vascular Plants

Earlier in this book the author stressed the point that seeds and other diaspores of vascular plants drifted to the shores of Surtsey and dispersed to the island by various other means shortly after it was formed and while the volcanoes were still active.

A number of seeds were collected on the shore in 1964 and proved viable and capable of germinating, although no vascular plant started growing during this first summer of the island's existence. But it was considered likely that pioneers of vascular plants would soon be found growing along the shore.

Fig 12.5. A flowering sea rocket.

Fig. 12.6. A lungwort on the Surtsey sand.

After searching the island thoroughly in the second summer, I discovered the first higher plant in 1965. Small seedlings of the sea rocket *Cakile edentula* were found growing upon the sandy beach north of the small lagoon on the island. During a later expedition in June that year, some 20 additional seedlings of the same species were discovered on the beach east of the previous location. The plants were all growing in a mixture of tephra and decaying thalli from the seaweed, *Ascophyllum nodosum*, which evidently formed a suitable medium for the germination and growth of the young plants, as the *Cakile* is apparently quite nitrophilous.

The plants had grown from seeds that obviously had been washed ashore, possibly along with the seaweed that might act as a float, aiding dispersal of seeds by ocean. The seedlings of these pioneer colonists, however, did not mature, and succumbed a few weeks later under a shower of ashes carried from the volcanic crater Syrtlingur. The fall of fresh tephra from this satellite volcano thus delayed the successful colonization of higher plants on Surtsey for one year.

The discovery of the *Cakile* plants on Surtsey

Fig. 12.7. A patch of sea sandwort. The species is the most common vascular plant on Surtsey.

showed that living seeds could be carried by sea at least 20 km, which is the distance from the island to Heimaey, the nearest colony of *Cakile* (Fig. 12.5). This species develops fruits that are capable of floating and can be carried by sea.

The second attempt of higher plants to invade Surtsey took place during the summer of 1966. In July four seedlings of sea lyme-grass *Leymus are-*

narius, as well as a seedling of sea rocket were found growing on the sandy shore on the northern side of the island. These plants grew from seeds that had apparently also dispersed by sea, as they were all found growing in a zone at the high-tide line. They were subjected to a similar fate as the plants that had made an attempt to colonize in the year before. This time, however, the colonizers were wiped out by ocean waves sweeping over the low and sandy beach.

The summer of 1967 was more favorable for colonization, and a third species attempted to invade the island. This was the sea sandwort *Honckenya peploides*, a common perennial on the southern shore of Iceland. During the summer, 26 individuals of this species were recorded, a number of which produced considerable vegetative growth. The colonization of the sea sandwort was decisive for the vegetation on Surtsey, as during the following years it spread out over the island and became the dominant member of the ecosystem.

The fourth species on the island was the oyster plant or the lungwort *Mertensia maritima* a perennial of which only one specimen was found on the "New Year" lava by the lagoon. Later some seeds of lungwort were also carried towards the lava on the eastern side of the island, and there a few plants developed. There on the sand covered lava is at present a small spot of ten sq. m grown with this pretty coastal species (Fig. 12.6).

During the same year the two former colonizers were also represented. A few plants of lymegrass were found on the sand and pebble-beach at the high-tide mark, as well as a few individuals of sea rocket that grew here and there on the ness, of which 15 flowered and six bore mature pods.

Plants of the sea rocket were thus the first to flower on the island. They set approximately 300 pods with twice as many seeds. The sea rocket was, therefore, first of the colonizers to succeed in multiplying in the new habitat and in laying the foundation for a new generation of plants on the island of Surtsey. It was therefore surprising that no sea rockets showed up in 1968. The reason for this is not known, but the species is an annual, and neither old plants nor the seed from the last year's crop seem to have survived.

Fig. 12.8. Scurvy grass in a lava crevice on Surtsey. Sea gulls likely carried the seed of this plant from nearby islands,

The sea sandwort plants, on the other hand, had increased in number and were now found growing farther up on the eastern lava, where they were better sheltered from the waves and wind in the sand-covered hollows (Fig. 12.7).

In 1969 still another vascular species was added to the island's flora. This was the scurvy grass *Cochlearia officinalis*, which is common to the coast of Iceland and is found on the skerries and larger islands in the Westman archipelago. Four plants belonging to this species were found growing near one of the plastic barrels filled with rain-water used to attract birds, this being the only source of fresh water on the island. These plants had obviously been carried as seed by birds to the barrels, and it was noted that the plants, beside the barrels, were growing out of bird droppings in association with the algae previously mentioned (Fig. 12.8). The total number of plants found on the island that year was reduced because of a rather unfavorable spring and summer.

In 1970, the major event was the discovery of still another vascular species; the common chickweed *Stellaria media*. Close scrutiny revealed that there were, in fact, four plants growing together in a compact bunch out of a sand-filled lava crack. Around them were fragments of shells, bird droppings and feathers, and it was obvious that the plants had grown up from the droppings of a bird. These plants matured and set

Fig. 12.9. A bladder-fern grows from a cavern in the Surtungur crater.

12 fruits. Some of the seeds ripened and dispersed from the plants during late summer.

An exceptionally large percentage of vascular plants survived the winter of 1970 to 1971, or 40 out of 75, and a few were added the following summer. Both that winter and spring were unusually mild, and as most of the plants had been growing in the rather sheltered parts of the ness and up on the lava edge to the east, they had a better chance to overwinter than individuals in previous years.

In extensive areas of the lava, an increased amount of tuff and ash had drifted in from the tephra mounds. At first the sand accumulation in the lava had mainly taken place in the old lava on the western side and consisted partly of tephra from the volcanic island of Jólnir, but gradually the lava became filled up by drifting sand from the eastern edge of the coastal plain as well as the tephra cone. This may to some extent explain the increased distribution of plants in the lava apron that took place in 1971.

During a detailed search for plants in the lava that year we came upon three small ferns that were growing down from a cave roof. These turned out to be small individuals of the bladder fern *Cystopteris fragilis*, the most common fern in Iceland, which grows both on the post-glacial lava as well as on other rocks and cliffs. The plants on Surtsey had reached two to three cm length when first observed and kept on developing, as they were sheltered and shaded from the direct sunlight (Fig. 12.9).

During the summer of 1971 there were 83 individuals of vascular plants on Surtsey, of which 49 survived the winter 1971-72, or close to 60%. This was an even higher percentage of sur-

Fig. 12.10. The see gulls probably carried seed of this saltmarsh-grass to the top of this lava rock.

viving individuals than the year before. The majority of the individuals that year were growing in the relatively secure sites of the lava, with fewer individuals on the northern ness than in previous years. This latter location is often over-flooded during winter storms and is thus quite hazardous for the overwintering of plants. Each year an increased number of plants survive the winter due to the more secure location of growth and a steady increase of perennial plants.

Until that time there had been an addition of approximately one new species of vascular plants to the island's flora every year since the colonization of these plants started. However, in 1972, at least four new species were discovered. These were: *Angelica archangelica, Carex maritima,* a *Puccinellia species,* and *Matricaria maritima.* All of these species are common on other islands in the Westman archipelago or on the lava flows of the mainland.

The *Angelica* species was represented by two small seedlings with the cotyledons and seed coat attached. They were growing at the high-tide mark on the north-eastern part of the ness, which indicated that the plants developed from seed that had drifted to Surtsey on the ocean from

Fig 12.12. A red fescue plant growing alone on the cinder substrate.

nearby islands, where the species is common. This colonization, however, did not last long, and it was not until 1997 that a new landing attempt was tried by that species.

A small grass like plant had been growing for some time on the lava east of the August crater. It was first incorrectly recorded in 1970 as a seedling of lyme-grass but was in 1972 definitely identified and listed as the curved sedge *Care maritime.* The plant had not produced any flower stalks, but it had developed stolons and was by

Fig, 12,11, The mayweed has occupied the area of the herring gull colony, Mávaból.

that time increasing vegetatively, so that several new individuals were being formed beside the mother plant. The sand filled lava on Surtsey is favorable for this *Carex* species, just as similar habitats are on the mainland, however, the species has not developed to any extent on the island.

The third new species in 1972 was the retroflexed saltmarsh-grass *Puccinellia distans*, which is common on other islands and skerries in the neighborhood. Two individuals representing this species were growing near one of the sites where a water container had been placed. This site, like the others where traps had been set up to catch fresh water micro-organisms, was frequently visited by birds. It is therefore very likely that these two plants also developed from seeds dispersed to the area by sea-gulls or other frequent bird visitors (Fig. 12.10).

The fourth new species discovered in that year was the mayweed *Matricaria maritima*, a very common species on all of the Westman Islands. The first plant of the species on Surtsey grew on the southern edge of the lava apron in a sand-covered hollow, which was also occupied by individuals of scurvy grass. It is likely that all the plants in the same hollow grew from seeds brought to the edge of the lava rocks by birds that often roost on these southern rocks or fly along the shore. Later the mayweed grew up in the Surtungur crater, where it flowered beautifully on the black pumice substrate, and eventually the species colonized the area on the southern lava occupied by the herring gulls (Fig. 12.11).

In 1973 the red fescue *Festuca rubra* became the newest addition to the Surtsey flora. The red fescue is the most common species in the neighboring islands, so it had been expected as an immigrant on Surtsey. To start with, only one plant succeeded in getting established in the sand filled lava at the centre of the island. In 1975 this plant had increased in size and was carrying a number of flowers. This grass plant, however, had some casualties, as it was torn up by a black-back sea gull that used it for nest building. Such ill luck can happen to individuals and hinder their progress of colonization.

A couple of times a few fescues have tried without success to settle on the western part of the island, but the first individual still survives (Fig. 12.12). Later on the fescue invaded the southern lava field, where it has become common.

Fig 12.13. The pearlwort has spread out over the southern part of the ropy lava.

In the year 1975 there were five new colonists of vascular plants on the island. One of the species that started to grow on the eastern part of the island was the arctic rush *Juncus arcticus*, which probably grew up from a seed brought to the island by a bird. This plant did not survive, but in 1990 there was a second attempt made by this species on the southern part of the island that became more successful.

That same summer a small plant of a bladder campion *Silene uniflora* was discovered on the northern ness. This plant survived there only for a short time, but in 1992 the species made another attempt higher up on the lava, and since then a few plants spread in two areas out over the cinder.

Yet another species arrived in the summer 1975. It was a field horsetail *Equisetum arvense*, which is common on sand-filled lava fields in Iceland. Two young plants had started to grow from their prothalli up near the Surtungur crater. The plants must have grown from spores that were brought by wind from the mainland. These two plants did not survive for long, but in 1990 new individuals were found growing at the same site.

The fourth species found in 1975 was a pearlwort *Sagina procumbens*. This was a small plant growing from seed brought by a bird up to the crater. It proved an unsuccessful attempt, but eleven years later the pearlwort played a major role as a pioneer. A number of plants then started to grow on a lava field at the southern side of the island, where the colony of sea gulls was breeding. The ropy lava is there relatively flat, and thus holds some moisture after rainy weather. There these plants prosper, especially as they are being fertilized by the numerous sea gulls that nest in this area (Fig. 12.13).

The fifth plant that colonized the island in 1975 was a common mouse-ear *Cerastium fontanum*, which is a common plant on gravelly and dry soils in Iceland. Seeds of this species have dispersed to Surtsey by a bird, as the plant was discovered in a depression south of the August crater. Although this species was rather slow in spreading, it has become permanent on Surtsey. Later a number of mouse-ear plants started to grow on the southern part of the island. On that spot were fifty individuals in 1992. The species is

Fig. 12.14. The sheep-sorrel covered an isolated spot on a flat, sand filled lava.

Fig. 12.15. Rock-cress on the cinder south of the Surtungur lava crater.

Fig. 12.16. A thrift. A raven had carried the seed to the island.

gradually increasing in number and distribution and has in places formed luxuriant colonies.

No new species was discovered the following summer, but a small atriplex plant was found in the high-tide zone of the northern ness two years later, in 1977. Seed of this *Atriplex longipes* plant was apparently carried by sea to the shore of Surtsey from the nearby islands, where this species grows in abundance as it also does on the mainland. That plant did not survive for long on the shore, as the ocean waves easily wash away organisms that try to settle upon the beach, but another specimen appeared on the island in 1996. The species has, however, not yet established a firm foothold on the island.

Fig. 12.17. A buttercup growing in a mat of sea sandwort out in the Mávaból.

Then in 1978 it was noticed, that on flat, sand-filled lava on the south-western part of the island, a small colony of sheep-sorrel *Rumex acetosella*, was covering a spot of one square metre. About one hundred plants occupied the area, some of which were flowering. The seeds of these plants were very likely brought to this spot by birds the previous year, as gulls frequently visit this place. The colony has since increased in size, but the species has not obtained a wide distribution on the island, although it has become a permanent resident (Fig.12.14).

It was furthermore noticed in 1978 that five rock-cress plants *Cardaminopsis petraea* were growing together south of the Surtungur lava crater. Obviously birds had carried the seed up to this lava shoulder. The seeds had germinated and developed to form these plants, which were flowering and forming seed capsules. The sand-filled lava has been a favorable substrate for the rock-cress, which is gradually spreading out from the pioneer plants (Fig. 12.15).

Two more additions of vascular plant species came to Surtsey in 1986. One of these was a thrift *Armeria maritima* that was found flowering on a rock shelf in the Surtungur crater. The plant was growing there among small sticks and string pieces that a raven had carried up to the ledge for nest making. The birds never completed the nest, though they succeeded in carrying the seed of this stately colonist. From this tuft some seed have later dispersed to the western side of the crater brim, where new plants of thrifts started growing (Fig. 12.16).

The other species discovered during the summer of 1986 was a smooth meadow-grass *Poa pratensis*, which apparently had been brought there by birds, as it was found growing beside a sea gull's nest. There the grass developed in the neighborhood of the nesting birds.

The following year two more grass species colonized the island. These were a few plants of annual meadow-grass *Poa annua* and one specimen of creeping bent-grass *Agrostis stolonifera*. Birds had carried both these species as seeds from the nearby island, where they are quite common. The annual meadow-grass has later spread out in the vicinity, as it receives fertilizer from the sea gulls. There the site has become rather fertile and suitable for this species.

During the years 1990 to 1992 there was an increase of nine species to the Surtsey community. These were mostly types that grow on dry meadowland and hayfields or on still more fertile areas of the mainland. They had all invaded the area of seagull breeding ground, which the birds keep fertile. Of each species there were only one or two individuals. In 1990 were recorded single individuals of shepherd's-purse *Capsella bursa-pastoris*, lady's-mantle *Alchemilla vulgaris*, marsh willow-herb *Epilobium palustre* and the wood rush *Luzula multiflora*. The following year three more species were discovered. These were knotweed *Polygonum aviculare*, dandelion *Taraxacum* spp and the common sorrel *Rumex acetosa*. And in the summer 1992 three more species were added to the island flora, such as buttercup *Ranunculus acris*, the common bent grass *Agrostis capillaris* and marsh foxtail *Alopecurus geniculatus* (Fig. 12.17). The following years both the sorrel and the foxtail increased their distribution, as the fertile lava field seemed to be a suitable substrate for these species.

During the summer 1993 four new species had occupied the western part of the bird-nesting area. These were tufted hairgrass of an Alaskan type *Deschampsia beringensis*, brown bentgrass *Agrostis vinealis*, spike rush *Eleocharis quinque-flora* and crowberry *Empetrum nigrum*. Noteworthy was to find the crowberry on the lava of Surtsey, as the species is not found growing on the outer islands. Birds must therefore have carried the berries quite a long way, possibly from Heimaey or even from the mainland.

In the following years several more species colonized the island. It was remarkable to find a least willow *Salix herbacea* growing in the lava of Surtsey in 1995 and later to find even two more willow species there, such as the tea leaved willow *Salix phylicifolia* in 1998 and then wooly willow *S. lanata* in 1999. These woody species are not found on the neighboring islands, and the seed of these plants very likely dispersed by air from the mainland.

During the past forty years in the history of Surtsey around 60 vascular plant species have started growth on the island. On the average at least one and a half new species per year have been added to the flora of Surtsey. Most of these are grasses or fell-field species. Lately there has been a steady increase of plants, but it cannot be expected that the increase continues as fast in the years to come, as many of the common species on the nearby islands have already colonized Surtsey. At this state, however, 13 % of the Icelandic vascular plant species have succeeded in colonizing Surtsey (Fig. 12.18).

Reproduction of Individuals

The sea lyme-grass

There has been a great increase in distribution of sea-lyme grass on Surtsey during the last years. To start with, new individuals of this species all derived from the seed that had drifted to the island. However, when the two oldest sea-lyme plants on the eastern side of Surtsey started maturing seed, there was a great change in the reproduction of plants of this species. The dispersal of lyme seed to Surtsey is small and rather unstable. During the first 14 years in the history of the island on the average only ten new sea-lyme plants started growth there annually. The seeds that may have arrived to the island could have been more numerous, but the death rate of seedlings could also have been high. Although the oldest sea-lyme plants started flowering in 1979 and bore mature seed, it was not until 1983 that young seedlings developed near the old mother plants.

During the summer 1982 there were 76 spikes on the two sea-lyme grass plants that flowered on Surtsey, and they developed around 4000 seeds. The following summer there were only 38 seedlings close to the mother plants. During the autumn of 1983 these same plants bore 240 spikes that produced 12 000 seeds. In the summer of 1984 there were 150 new seedlings in the same area. It may thus be concluded that only 1% of the maturing seed will form seedlings that manage to develop. To start with, the increase of sea-lyme grass was slow, as it took five to seven years for the plants to flower and produce seed. The second and third generations have now come into production and an increase of plants can be expected. The growth conditions are favorable, and there are wide areas of sand-filled lava that can be occupied by the species. The sea-lyme grass could thus become a dominant plant on the eastern part of Surtsey.

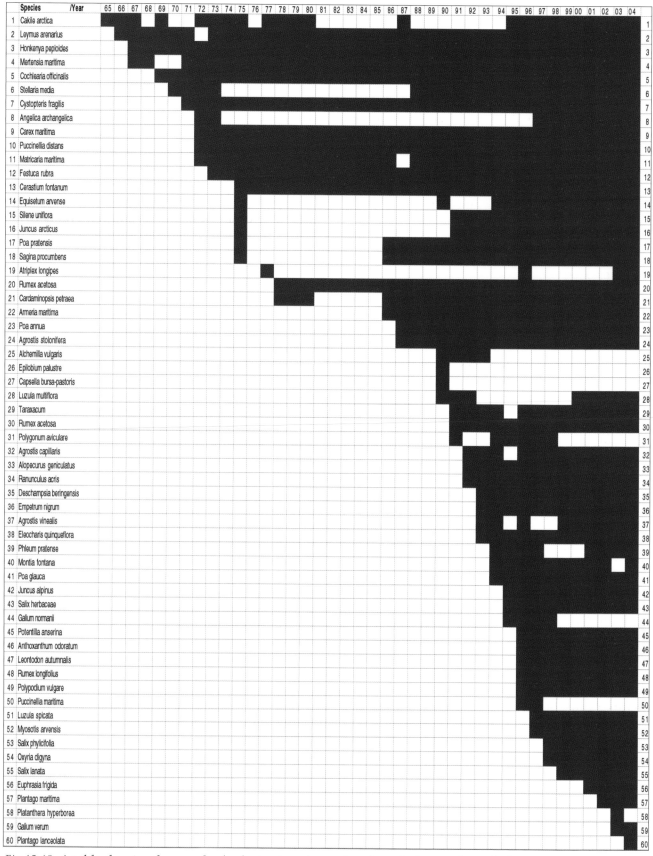

Fig 12.18. A table showing the records of colonization of vascular plants in Surtsey from the beginning.

82

The sea sandwort

The first five years after the sea sandwort plant was discovered on Surtsey the increase of that species depended exclusively on seed that could drift by sea, and would be washed upon the shore of the island. Annually there was an increase of some 20-30 plants, but half of these colonists were lost every winter, due to sand drift, surf action and other casualties. The older plants gradually increase in size and spread out over the sand, where they form disk shaped patches, which can become two to three metres wide. It takes these plants five to seven years to become fertile, after which time they can produce a great number of seeds.

The sea sandwort became fertile on Surtsey in 1971 and five years later, a plant was found producing 1000 seedpods. Still later on it was noticed that a plant could even form 50 000 seed per summer. Although only one or two seeds out of hundred succeed in developing a plant, it is obvious that the species can multiply rapidly. In reality plants on Surtsey produced several hundreds of seedlings per year, when they finally became fertile. The second generation of sandworts became mature on the island in 1977 and since then there has been a steady increase of the species.

At present the distribution of the sea sandwort continues, and the patches can enlarge to a certain point. Twelve-year-old plants can cover an area of five square metres. Measurements show that the sandwort covers over 10% of the cinder ground on Surtsey, and that in a sand filled hollow south of the shelter on the island the cover exceeds 60% of the ground. Thus the sea sandwort may be considered the leading colonist on Surtsey.

Carex maritima

Plants multiply by spores or seeds but they can also propagate vegetatively.

The development of the curved sedge *Carex maritima*, may be taken as an example of the establishment of a colony by vegetative propagation. The species is common on the sands and volcanic soils of the southern mainland, whence diaspores may have been brought to Surtsey by geese that feed on this species.

A single plant started growing in 1970, quite isolated on the central part of the island where the substrate was sand-filled lava. The propagation from the mother plant has been followed closely. Propagules were formed by the mother plant and gave rise to new individuals. The length of rhizomes restricts the distribution of the individuals in this colony. Thus the area occupied by the new vegetative plant population was much smaller than that formed through seed distribution. When the daughter plants in turn start propagating, their offspring will not enjoy the same freedom of space as the first generation, and there will be an increased and an uneven competition between individuals of the population.

Communities

The lyme-grass sand dune, coastal community

As previously mentioned sea lyme-grass was one of the first pioneers on Surtsey. The colonists distribute by seed and stolons. Since 1974 two sea lyme-grass plants have been growing on a lava edge at the eastern side of the island. They annually developed rhizomes so that the plants increase in size and gradually form a large mat. The growing site is sand-filled lava. As the sand is constantly moving, it drifts into the vegetation mat, where it falls among the straws, and gradually builds up a dune, which becomes higher and larger as the plant increases in size. The development of one of these dunes has been monitored. Its area now measures 10 x 5.5 m and the height is around 1.5 metres.

In the vicinity of the sea lyme-grass there were some sea sandwort-plants. As these plants increased in size, their territory started to overlap, thus these two species plus a lungwort *Mertensia maritima* have developed into a primitive coastal community that has been studied closely. This was the first community of vascular plants formed in Surtsey.

Here the sandwort serves as a pioneer plant holding the ground stratum, protecting the plants from the drifting sand and enjoying the light during the spring months. The lyme-grass, with its high stem and long leafs, stretches above the sandwort, taking advantage of the moist sand media held in place by that species.

This dune association is typical for colonies that are formed when two ore more plants of different species twine together by vegetative growth as they spread out over a common territory (Fig. 12.19). There are, however, other means to produce such associations, as was also demonstrated by these two species on Surtsey.

In the neighborhood of the large lyme-grass plants a number of sandwort patches had been established. It was then noticed in the summer of 1983 that in the centre of some of these patches a young lyme-grass plant was developing. The large lyme-grass plants had matured seed the year before and the seeds were distributed in the vicinity. Some were blown away by winter storms, they had fallen into the ocean or on the solid lava and others had been buried too deep in the sand or withered on its dry surface and had not succeeded in developing into a new seedling. The lyme-grass seeds that landed in sandwort patch in contrast encountered more favorable conditions. Such seed were not buried too deep in sand, but received an even supply of moisture and were better sheltered than on open sand. This special microhabitat had obviously been favorable for the sprouting of lyme-grass seeds, since seedlings of twenty lyme-grass plants were found in the centre of the same number of sandwort patches, whereas no new seedlings had been developing in the sand around these patches.

The following year, in the summer of 1984, this tendency had increased, and lyme-grass plants were found in sandwort patches growing at a distance of 350 m from the seed-bearing lyme-grass plant. During the following years an increasing number of such coexistence was noted, as the sandwort had provided a favorable habitat for the lyme-grass. In 1992 the lyme-grass was occupying over 10% of all the sandwort patches in an area of the eastern part of Surtsey.

The pearlwort-Gull bed

In the history of Surtsey's biota a marked step was taken, when on the fairly smooth surface of the ropy *aa* lava on the southern part of the island in quadrat R-14, a colony of the procumbent pearlwort *Sagina procumbens* plants began developing in 1986. As previously indicated, the plants had been growing there the year before and had obviously been carried as seeds by the gulls that had started breeding at the place. On the flat lava surface the plants could collect moisture from the rain and keep the spot fairly wet when other parts of the lava had dried out.

At the edge of the spot was also a small patch of reflexed saltmarsh-grass *Puccinellia distans*, which also had grown up from seed brought with the gulls' dung. Originally there were some 150 pearlwort plants spread out in a thin net on the lava shelf, but in two years this number was tenfold. In the breeding grounds of the gulls there was also a rapid increase of nests, which were lined with a moss carpet. The birds brought seafood to their chicks but left offal and guano by the nests and in their vicinity.

At the northern edge of this lava spot were two new grass species growing in 1987. There a few plants of creeping bent-grass *Agrostis stolonifera* were developing small oasis and to that seed of the annual meadow-grass *Poa annua* had been transported.

The herring gulls continued to carry seeds and fertilizer to the area and its neighborhood, thus there has been a steady increase of plant species on this site, which is named Mávaból (The Gull Bed). In 1998 there were twenty species of vascular plants within the area of the total of 47 species found at that time on the whole island. The vegetation there covered on the average 72% of the lava and sandy substrate, and the soil had obtained a pH 6.4 compared with the more neutral substrate of pH 7.5 outside the colony.

This colony covers an increasing area in the lava field, and is becoming more fertile as the gull population gets bigger. There, an association is developing that is very similar to any assortment in a barnyard flora or at the edge of a hayfield. To that spot had the mayweed *Matricaria maritima* been carried as well as the scurvy-grass *Cochlearia officinalis*, that had previously been found growing both at the edge of the lava and farther up on the island, but were at this site enjoying a more fertile habitat. Following this, some plants of chickweed *Stellaria media* started growth among the grasses, and in 1991 both sorrels and dandelions were ornamenting the lava hollows just as they were growing at the edge of a fertile hayfield.

The following year this same habitat was also occupied by a buttercup *Ranunculus acris* that displayed there its beautiful yellow flowers on the black lava fields, where it grew among the marsh foxtails *Alopecurus geniculatus,* which had invaded the lava field along with other colonists.

In this area a colony of nitrophilous species were in development following a totally different trend from the usual plant societies on Icelandic lava fields. There a specific island vegetation is in development, an important ecosystem for the biota of Surtsey (Fig. 12.20).

> *During the first years of the colonization of life on Surtsey there was little competition among individuals, as there was plenty of barren land to occupy on the vastness of the island. But to study the ability of the species to colonize the various habitats and to follow its success in the colony proved to be an interesting project. The species prosper in the mixed society only if they are well situated and have good means of sustenance, which are light, food, water and growing space. The individuals fight for these necessities in their habitat, and the individual suffers, which is deprived of such benefits, but various parasites can also hinder its development. By studying the conditions the individual requires for growth and development, and its use of the riches offered by the habitat one may define the niche it occupies in the ecosystem. On Surtsey the pioneers had the advance over others in the colonization, if they were able to reproduce and disperse, but the coexistence with other individuals in the colony can either be harmful to them or beneficial.*

Terrestrial Animals

So far there has not been a great deal of organic matter produced by the terrestrial vegetation on Surtsey, and the producers have thus not been able to support any substantial amount of life occupying higher tropic levels. Most of the animals observed on Surtsey are therefore visitors that obtain their energy from sources not directly belonging to the island's ecosystem. A few of the animals may be considered partial occupants, and some have reproduced on the island although their food is sought away from their breeding site.

Fig. 12.19. A dune is gradually being built up, as sand drifts into the sea lime grass colony. The dune gradually increases in height.

Fig. 12.20. At the sea gull area, Mávaból, the vegetation flourishes. The August Crater is to the left and The Eastern Cone, Austur Bunki, in background.

Still, a smaller number of individuals may be listed as permanent colonizers of Surtsey.

Microfauna

In the surface tephra just above the high-tide line marine algae are washed up with the ocean spray. There this organic matter is used as food by bacteria, fungi, and a few lower animals. In 1968 this substrate was sampled and an analysis performed to determine whether species of lower animals were present and to investigate their composition and abundance.

Fig. 12.21. Collecting insects from the glue trap. Slimy cylinders were used in Surtsey as traps for flying insects. Daily a number of insects were collected and stored for further identifications.

The tephra samples were examined microscopically for amoebae, testacea, flagellates, and ciliates. This was performed after a 2-3 g portion of the tephra had been spread out on agar plates with different culture media and an addition of the bacterium *Aerobacter*, which was used as a food source. This examination revealed that only flagellated protozoa were present. The quantitative determination of the individuals showed that there were on the average only 290 flagellates in a gram of tephra. This is a much lower number than would be found in the soil of a highly developed grassland community. These flagellated protozoa may be pioneer species of the Surtsey substrate. They can easily disperse to the island by wind, being carried on or with dust particles. They may be the first to appear, as these species have lighter spores than most other protozoa. Above the high-tide mark these organisms find their appropriate food source, and in this habitat they become the primary consumers in the ecosystem.

Higher up on the island, near fumaroles and other moist spots in the Surtur craters where algae and moss have gradually established their first colonies, the microfauna may find adequate food supply, and there the various airborne spores dispersing to the island have a fair chance of developing.

In 1970 some of these locations were visited and samples taken from patches of algae and moss growing in lava caves and on edges of fumaroles with moist surfaces formed by the con-densed steam. After culturing the vegetation samples on nutrient media of a solid or liquid substrate, different hardy microzoa were discovered, individuals belonging to amoebae and ciliates, as well as two species of bdelloid rotifers.

All of these forms are considered to be cosmopolitans and capable of reproducing asexually. The animals are readily transformed into resting forms and can in this stage be transported to the island. These microzoa are all capable of withstanding severe environmental changes such as drought and frost. It is therefore clear that they are capable of being the pioneer consumers at the lower trophic level of the food chain in the moist lava habitat on Surtsey, where they feed on the blue-green algae, *Nostoc*, and bacteria.

Terrestrial Invertebrates

It should be pointed out that already in 1971 two nematodes; *Acrobeloides nanus* and a species of *Monhystera*, were discovered on the island, although these individuals were obtained from the rather artificial habitat of the fresh water container so often mentioned in previous chapters of this book. At least the former species is comparable to other animals so far observed in the micro-fauna of Surtsey with respect to reproduction, distribution, and the ability to withstand severe environmental conditions. The *A. nanus* nematode is parthenogenetic and has the ability to survive desiccation, so that these individuals can, better than many other animals, endure drought and thus successfully manage to disperse to Surtsey. They are bacteria feeders, and occupy a very low trophic level.

It was a remarkable event when the first earthworms were discovered on Surtsey in 1993. This first introduction was *Lumbricus castaneus*, a species known to occupy the neighboring islands. Two juvenile individuals of the species were found in the soil of the gull colony. Most likely they have dispersed by birds from the other islands or from the mainland of Iceland.

The first specimen of terrestrial invertebrates discovered on Surtsey was, however, a diptera fly, later identified as that of *Diamesa zernyi*. This fly was collected in 1964 on the western shore during the first spring of Surtsey's existence, only half a year after the island was first formed.

The following summer five more specimens of flies and midges were collected, as well as two species of moths and the mite *Thinoseius spinosus*. It was especially interesting to note that the mite was apparently living on some dead *Heleomyza borealis*, which is a common fly on neighboring islands. Thus, a food chain was already established, from the carcass, to the mite, and ending in a mould that was found living on one of the dead mites.

In 1966 glue-traps were set up on the island to capture flying insects, and a systematic collection of terrestrial Arthropods commenced (Fig. 12.21). During that year 22 species of insects were recorded and four species of Arachnida. Since then a number of new species of Arthropods are recorded every year that passes. In the year 1967 some 56 species of Insecta and seven species of Arachnida were collected and in 1968 there was an addition of eight new species. In the years 1969 and 1970 the number had increased to 112 species of Insecta and 24 of Arachnida.

Many species of butterflies and moths *Lepidoptera* have so far been recorded on Surtsey. In 1965 we discovered a specimen of the silver-Y moth *Autographa gamma*, which is not native to Iceland but migrates from the mainland of Europe or from the British Isles. This moth and other Lepidoptera are excellent flyers and migrate over long distances on their own wing support.

All the insects discovered on Surtsey were winged, but it is doubtful that they could have managed to reach the island if they were not also aided by favorable winds. It has, for example, been noted that during strong northerly winds, the number of airborne individuals has increased markedly. Most of the 80 Diptera species are, as a result of this, considered to have reached Surtsey by these means of dispersal. Ballooning of spiders is one way of dispersal, which is aided by wind. In 1966 a small living spider of the family Linyphiidae was discovered on the northern ness of the island. This spider had apparently been ballooning on the long thread that was secreted by the animal, especially during the immature stage.

On a few occasions it has been possible to demonstrate that insects may be transported to Surtsey by sea. Such may have been the dispersal of the mite *Oribotritia faeroensis*, which was discovered on the island in 1966. The eleven individuals of this species were found alive on a gate-pole, which very likely had drifted to the island from the dumps on Heimaey. These mites later spread out into various areas on the island and in 1995 there were 22 species of Oribatid mites found on Surtsey, two of which may have derived from North America. In a similar way the weevil, *Otiorhynchus arcticus*, must have been carried to the island, as it is not able to fly. It is abundant on Heimaey and could have been transported by some kind of floats, but hardly by direct transport in the ocean, as experiments have shown that it does not survive immersion in water for more than 24 hours. This weevil, however, has not been a successful colonist on Surtsey. Other members of the soil fauna may as well have been brought by birds.

It was demonstrated during the bird collection that a number of birds were carrying insects on the exterior of their bodies, and even in their alimentary tracts, but some insects are also found to have mites, Acari, in their nymphal stage as parasites, and in that way have transported mites to the island.

Although there are strict regulations regarding the import of plants and animals to Surtsey, man has brought at least two flies, *Drosophila funebris* and *Musca domestica*, to the island. These two species were found inside the scientists' hut and were very likely transported along with the provisions.

Origin and Colonization

The immigrating invertebrates collected thus far on Surtsey have mostly derived from the other islands of the archipelago. The insect fauna of these islands was consequently investigated in 1968, so that it is now possible to determine which of the animals hitherto found on Surtsey could have derived from these islands while also recording the shortest possible distance of dispersal. Heimaey being the largest of the islands, also has the greatest number of invertebrate species and has, very likely, supplied Surtsey with a number of immigrants although it lies farther away than many of the smaller islands.

It has also been demonstrated that some of the individuals found on Surtsey must have come from the mainland of Iceland, as no representatives of the same species are found on the

Westman Islands. Many of the active flyers, such as some of the Noctuid moths and the butterflies, must even have derived from the mainland of Europe, as they are not native to Iceland. These individuals have therefore dispersed over the Atlantic with air-currents and finally landed on the island.

It must be kept in mind that the greatest number of individuals belonging to the various species of terrestrial invertebrates so far found on Surtsey are only casual visitors that happen to be carried to the island and have little chance of survival. Only a small number have been able to survive for any length of time, and only a few of these have been able to breed and may be considered to have become temporary or permanent inhabitants.

The number of arthropods already recorded on Surtsey may be considered high in relation to the total number known in Iceland. Out of the 1250 species known to be established on the mainland (Acaria excluded), 240 have been collected on Surtsey, which indicates that the dispersal of arthropods to the island must be relatively easy. In addition 62 species of acarids have been recorded from Surtsey, hitherto a neglected group on the mainland. As stated earlier, there are several means of transport for the various terrestrial invertebrates: by own wing support, by wind, water, on various floats, by other animals, or man.

The main hindrance to a successful colonization was to start with the lack of available food supply for the animals in this new habitat, as the vegetation was, until recently, not producing any substantial amount of organic matter. The major food source was then the organic matter washed ashore from the sea. Insects that can breed and rear their offspring on such carcasses therefore had the best chance to colonize. Later many more species of terrestrial invertebrates have occupied the vegetative areas on the dry land of Surtsey.

In 1965 the fly *Heleomyza borealis* was discovered and later found to be breeding abundantly in carcasses of fish and birds on the coast of Surtsey. Since then this fly has been breeding periodically on the island, but its survival depends on the availability of food, and sea-gulls are hard competitors, devouring rapidly any carcasses washed upon the shore, so food is not permanently available. A safer place for this fly is in the gull breeding area farther up on the island. It lays eggs in the nests, and the maggots prosper in the fertile bottom of the bird nests.

The first collembola *Archisotoma besselsi* was discovered on Surtsey in 1967. It spreads easily with the sea currents along the coast of Iceland and has apparently been dispersed on the ocean surface to Surtsey, where it colonized the beach in the first years and found food under the driftwood and seaweed debris. The species has not been rediscovered in recent years. At least four collembola species were then permanent inhabitants of the island.

Before 1978 some 16 species of collembola had been found and in 1995 additional 9 species were recorded. At this time the greatest number were discovered in the gull breeding area on the southern part of the lava field, but most of the species discovered earlier had then disappeared.

In 1970 a chironomid midge *Halocladius variabilis* was found breeding in shallow pools at the tidal zone on Surtsey. This midge is common on Heimaey and it is reasonable to assume that it has become a permanent resident on Surtsey.

All these individuals are finding enough food sources on the beach and are capable of surviving and reproducing in the coastal habitat of the island, but farther inland the food source was scarce during the first years. Later, however as the vegetation increases many invertebrates have had a good chance to colonize. Thus the aphid *Acyrthosiphon auctus* feeds on the numerous sea sandwort plants, which are widespread all over the island. Similarly various Diptera live on the chickweed patches and the moss cover in moist places of crevices and caves.

By now there is enough food being supplied for predators like spiders that prey on other invertebrates. Some of these like *Erigone arctica* have become quite common and spread their webs and snares out over the moss-covered lava.

Individuals of the various groups of invertebrates have become legal inhabitants of the Surtsey' society. Thus there already exist on the island differently advanced ecosystems in which invertebrates are participants in the food web. They live there on the product of various plants and animals, and may in turn become the prey of birds.

Birds

Gulls were among the first living creatures to set foot on Surtsey, and they have continued to soar about its beaches and roost on its hills and cliffs ever since. The ocean around the Westman Islands is extremely rich in marine life used by various birds as a source of food. Gulls and waders feed on carcasses of marine animals cast ashore on the island, or make their catch from the ocean farther out and sometimes bring their prey on to dry land to devour it there. The remnants of such carcasses may, in turn, serve as an energy source for lower forms of life.

The presence of gulls on the island also greatly affects the future soil of Surtsey by their excreta, supplying fertilizer containing both minerals and organic matter. This was at first mainly deposited along the edge of the cliffs of the southern coast, on the sandy beach of the northern ness and on high peaks of the tephra cones. Later, when the gulls started breeding on the island, there became a marked change on the southern part of the lava, as the birds had a great effect by spreading droppings and various offals over the vegetative area. As previously mentioned, the birds have played their part in transporting diaspores of plants to Surtsey and are even carriers of various invertebrates. The birds are therefore very important members of the island's ecosystem, but until the present time they have mostly had to rely upon energy sources obtained from outside the boundaries of the island.

From the very beginning of the Surtsey research various observations were performed with regard to birds visiting the island. Records have been made, by skilled bird-watchers, of birds seen since the formation of the island. And during certain periods in early spring and autumn, birds have been collected for closer examination by ornithologists. In the spring migratory birds fly north from the continent of Europe and the British Isles, frequently visiting Surtsey, which is the first possible landing place for a number of these birds after crossing the Atlantic. In the autumn the birds have a reverse route when flying south from Greenland or the mainland of Iceland, and they may have a short visit to Surtsey. During such a visit the birds sometimes empty their guts and deposit seeds with their excreta. A flock of geese has been seen in flight over the island, bombing it with their droppings as they became disturbed by the presence of man on the island.

During the autumn, Iceland is often visited by drift migrants from northern Europe or Siberia making their journey south by the west coast of Europe and drift off their course across the Atlantic. Many of such stragglers that have been seen or caught on Surtsey may also be carriers of seeds, which are abundantly available at this time of the year. The ornithological work on Surtsey has been important in demonstrating the exact time of arrival of the various migrants to Iceland, their physical condition after their flight across the ocean, the part they may play in transporting other organisms, as well as their exodus in the autumn.

The kittiwake *Rissa tridactyla* may have been the first of the gulls to alight on the island during intervals between eruptions, and in 1964 a flock of these birds frequently rested on the tephra bluffs on the northern side, or on vertical lava cliffs that had been formed on the southern side of the island. Following the first visit of the gulls a group of redwings *Turdus iliacus* were seen in the early spring of 1964. In May the same year snow buntings *Plectrophenax nivalis* were observed upon the lava and a few purple sandpipers *Calidris maritima* and oystercatchers *Haemotopus ostralegus* feeding on the euphausids that had been washed ashore on the northern side of the island. The birds most frequently seen, however, were and still are the gulls.

The great black-backed gull *Larus marinus* occupied the flat sandy beach as well as the sand filled lava higher up on the southern part of the island. The herring gull *Larus argentatus* and the glaucous gull *Larus hyperboreus* also frequented that part. The arctic tern *Sterna paradisaea* used the flat sandy beach to rest on during its visit both in spring and autumn.

In early August during the first summer a large flock of rednecked phalaropes *Phalaropus lobatus* was swimming close to the shore. In October a single turtle dove *Streptopelia turtur* was then seen on the lava flow on the south-western part of the island. This last species occasionally drifts off course and could be one of the best carriers of seeds, when flying with a full crop to the island.

In 1965 a pair of ravens *Corvus corax* occasionally visited the island and was seen there frequently in the following years. The pair repeatedly built nests in the Surtungur crater without ever using them for egg laying.

In 1966 a total of 23 bird species were recorded as seen on the island, among which was a merlin *Falco columbarius* that flew over the lava in search of prey, which may have been the wheatear *Oenanthe oenanthe* or meadow pipits *Anthus pratensis* that were observed there at that time. These birds in turn may have been feeding on insects that obtained their energy source from plants that are at a still lower trophic level.

In 1967 there were 29 species of migratory birds observed on or around Surtsey, besides the 13 species of resident sea-birds that frequently occupy the neighboring islands. Among these were redshanks *Tringa totanus* and golden plovers *Pluvialis apricaria* in addition to several species of geese that either flew over the island or settled on the plains of the northern ness. One long-eared owl *Asio otus* was caught in the lava that spring, where it was apparently seeking some prey. This was available in abundance among the exhausted passerine migrants such as the white wagtail *Motacilla alba* that was frequently seen catching flies around the scientists' hut.

The following year 1968, a whooper swan *Cygnus cygnus* visited the island, and shortly thereafter a carcass of a swan was found on the beach, which blow-flies were attacking. The island was also visited by several ducks; such as mallards *Anas platyrhynchos*.

Among birds observed on the island in 1969 was a squacco heron *Ardeola ralloides*. This bird was new to Iceland. Such a discovery could be expected, as Surtsey is situated farther south than any other part of Iceland and the stragglers are most common in the autumn on the southern shores of the country. During this same summer nine other drift migrants were encountered. Among them were a European robin *Erithacus rubecula* and a jackdaw *Corvus monedula*.

In the year 1970 a number of new visitors were spotted on the island such as a corncrake *Crex crex*, a willow warbler *Phylloscopus trochilus* and a redstart *Phoenicurus phoenicurus*; and with every passing year the number of bird species seen on the island increases. Of more than 360 species of birds having been recorded in Iceland, 85 species have already been found on or around Surtsey.

Most of the drift migrants are only sporadic rarities that do not play any major role in the island's ecosystem unless they carry with them some rare plant materials. The major influence is without doubt exerted by the local sea-birds and the great populations of migrants that fly across the island regularly every spring and autumn.

Migratory birds coming from Iceland may pass over Surtsey towards the south, where they winter. In the spring the route is reversed: the migrating birds head north and many end up crossing Surtsey as they arrive in Iceland. Much information pertaining to migration routes has been accumulated by bird ringing, but thorough studies on the time of arrival and exodus of these birds by direct observation methods were also carried out in Surtsey.

As Surtsey lay in the path of the migrating birds, it was considered to fulfil requirements for studying their travel. The island was therefore manned by experienced bird-watchers, both in spring and autumn from 1967 to 1970. They observed the migration of birds and kept records of all birds seen on the island and in its vicinity. The main stream of migrants arrives at the south-eastern part of Iceland, leaving Surtsey somewhat off the direct route. During side-winds arriving birds may, however, in some years drift in great numbers to the island. The redwing and the golden plover are early arrivers and are followed after mid-April by various waders, such as turnstones *Arenaria interpres*, which were often seen by the hundreds during their stop-over on Surtsey. In late April and the first days of May geese and various small passerines may visit the island in large numbers.

During the migration studies about 200 individuals of some 20 bird species were collected each year. The smaller passerines had sometimes barely made the journey across the Atlantic due to unfavorable winds, and landed quite exhausted on Surtsey. This could be observed by the general appearance of the birds and demonstrated by measuring the shortage of fat deposits which birds use on their overseas crossings. Such conditions were especially noticeable in the case of wheatears that apparently sometimes proceed with a continuous migration flight from West Africa to Iceland. The ornithological work on Surtsey, furthermore, consisted of weighing and sexing the collected birds, as well as searching closely for any seeds that the birds might be carrying in their alimentary tract.

The greatest ornithological event, however, took place in the summer of 1970, when the first birds started nesting. These were seabirds of species common to the Westman Islands, i.e. the fulmar *Fulmarus glacialis* and the black guillemot *Cepphus grylle*. The former had built a nest on a ledge 10 m above sea-level in the cliffs on the western side of the island, whereas the latter had built its nest in a crevice in the lava rock on the south-west side. A year later there were seven black guillemots, and the birds continue to use the cliffs for nesting. Both nests were successful and birds of both of these species are now breeding permanently on the island, with their colonies becoming an integral part of the island's ecosystem, although they have to obtain their food and feed their young with the catch from nearby ocean (Fig 12.22).

Later the fulmar started nesting on the cliffs of the cinder cones, as well as in crevasses of the lava farther up on the island. In 2003 the fulmar colony had some 350 pairs nesting on Surtsey (Fig 12.23).

In 1974 greater black-backed gull *Larus marinus* nested in the lava field upon the island. The pair succeeded in bringing up one young. In following years, this same nest was occupied by these birds, but the black-backed gull also started nesting in several other areas of the island. In 1976 a pair of great black-backs used a patch of sea-sandwort for their nest. This location must have been quite favorable as the pair succeeded in raising three chicks in this sheltered place. But the plant also benefited as it obtained fertilizer and developed greatly that summer. The great black-backs also used the lyme grass communi-

Fig. 12.22. Black guillemots use the sea cliffs for breeding. In 1990 15 pairs of guillemots laid eggs in Surtsey.

Fig. 12.23. *A young fulmar in a nest, upon the edge of one of the craters. There were more than 350 breeding pairs of fulmars in Surtsey in 2003.*

Kittiwakes, the first birds to arrive, however, did not nest until about 1975, when they nested on the cliffs at the southern edge of the island. In that first year eight pairs of birds nested there in a group, but only four of the chicks fledged. The kittiwake is a sociable bird, however in this case, only as few as eight pairs of birds were needed to establish a breeding colony at a new location. The kittiwake has ever since used the cliffs for breeding, and in 2003 there were 130 nests on the island. The kittiwake is a common bird on Surtsey, and they frequently use the northern ness for resting. Sometimes there are hundreds or even thousands of birds sitting there in flocks (Fig.12.24). These are possibly young birds that have little association with the breeding birds on the southern part of the island.

On the northern sand spit large flocks of arctic terns may be seen in the autumn. But it also happened that a tern has laid an egg there on the sand. This first took place in 1975, but was repeated during the two following summers. One or a few eggs were laid, but the birds did not succeed in hatching them.

Then came the lesser black-backed gull *Larus*

ties on the sand dunes on the eastern side of the island for nesting and for sheltering their young. The lyme grass there also benefitted from the presence of the birds.

In 1978 there were six great black-back nests at various sites on the lava, and since then a slow increase in the breeding has taken place, so that in 2002 there were 35 nests of black-backs on the island.

Fig. 12.24. *A flock of kittiwakes on the northern spit of Surtsey in 1977.*

Fig. 12.25. The herring gull has become a common breeding bird in Surtsey. In building the nest it collects moss and parts of other plants from nearby islands.

fuscus and nested first on Surtsey in 1981 (Fig. 12.25), followed by the herring-gull *Larus argentatus,* that nested in 1985. These gulls have increased in numbers, so that over 150 nesting pairs were there on the southern part of the lava apron in the summer of 2003. It was furthermore noticed that one pair of glaucous gull *Larus hyperboreus* nested among the other gulls on Surtsey in 1993. And in 2002 there was still one nesting pair of this species on the island.

Eleven species of birds are now permanently nesting on the island. The most recent addition have been the snow bunting, white wagtail, grey lag goose *Anser anser* and meadow pipit.

The snow bunting was the first of the landbirds to start nesting on the island, when two pairs were found there in 1996. And in 2003 there were 10 pairs breeding on Surtsey. During the summer 1999 it was noticed that a pair of grey lag geese had been on the island, and since 2002 they have raised young. In 2001 a pair of white wagtail was first seen with young by the scientist's hut, and since then one pair has probably annually nested on the island, but a nest was first discovered in 2003. The meadow pipit is the most recent addition to the bird community on Surtsey, as two pairs were first discovered nesting there in 2003.

The lack of food sources from the producers or primary consumers of the ecosystem at first hindered colonization of land birds, and the nesting of such birds could hardly begin to take place until enough food was available in the form of seed or insects. And only when enough vegetation was available could the grey lag goose start breeding. Such birds as the raven, which can make use of carcasses drifting ashore and can live on robbing the nests of gulls, could be expected to colonize the island, but that bird has not yet succeeded in laying eggs on Surtsey.

Of all these birds, the gulls have had the greatest impact on the island. Their nests are foci of pioneering by lower life forms, worms and insects, and at their breeding area the birds annually carry new plant material and fertilize diverse communities of plants with their droppings and offal.

13. Development

"And now, if you have anything more to ask, I can't think how you can manage it, for I've never heard anyone tell more of the story of the world. Make what use of it you can."

(The Deluding of Gylfi)

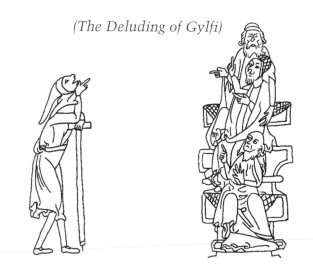

Studies of the Adjacent Landmasses

One of the factors affecting colonization of terrestrial organisms on Surtsey is the available sources of species on the adjacent landmasses. As a background for evaluating the colonization of plants and animals on the new island, a good knowledge of the biota of the neighboring landmasses is a prerequisite. In the manual of vascular plants of Iceland records are made of some species of vascular plants growing in the Westman Islands as well as the various locations on the adjacent mainland. In order to establish better knowledge of the flora in this area, however, it was considered necessary for the Surtsey studies to carry out an investigation of the vegetation of these areas. These studies fall into three groups: The outer Westman Islands, Heimaey, and the South coast of Iceland.

A thorough study of the marine algae on the various islands and the southern shore of Iceland has also been performed. Similarly the marine fauna in the archipelago is getting fairly well known through various biological research work. In addition to this the entomologists have investigated the terrestrial invertebrates of the different islands as well as on the southern mainland. Furthermore, the bird life of these areas has been under a continuous scrutiny.

Besides this, the geological examinations of the Westman Islands have also received great attention by the geologists who continue their research of the area. Thus the volcanic origin and development of the islands are by now rather well understood.

Oceanographic phenomena are under routine observation, and similarly there are permanent meteorological recordings carried out in the area. Thus the Westman Islands have awakened the interest of scholars of various disciplines who have accumulated great knowledge about life and its environment in the archipelago.

Colonization and Development

Of the vast number of species hitherto arriving on Surtsey, only a limited number have been able to establish themselves. Many spores and seeds have germinated without further success of growth, and consumers have found a negligible amount of food sources on the island to survive on. For most of the organisms attempting colonization, it has been a hard struggle for existence. Although the dispersal has been quite restricted, the highly specialized and stringent environmental conditions present on Surtsey have chiefly governed the strict natural selection of pioneers.

A successful colonization, however, does not take place unless the conditions are favorable on the island for the new arrival, so that it can withstand the limitations extended by the edaphic and climatic factors. So far, little competition is

Fig. 13.1. The dry sand and the porous lava are difficult substrates for colonization of any organism.

Fig. 13.2. The sea sandwort has a widespread root system and can collect moisture and nutrition from a large area.

taking place between the newly invaded plants on most of the dry land of Surtsey. But the conditions on the island have been so stringent that only the most tolerant species have succeeded in getting established (Fig. 13.1 and 13.2).

Surtsey has sandy beaches containing organic material, washed ashore by the ocean, such as seaweed and the remains of birds and marine organisms. Although these beaches are unstable habitats, they were more favorable for an invasion than the dry lava and the scouring tephra.

The ocean around the island is an obvious barrier to the dispersal of dry land plants, but it was at first the main route of transport for seed of various coastal plants. Such seed is constantly being washed upon the shores, and it was inevitable that some coastal plants would be among the first pioneers. Thus the ocean favoured the colonization on the beach to a greater extent than on inland lava and tephra, but the pioneers on the beach are also subject to the great erosive effect of the ocean on their habitat, and are, therefore, less protected and not as stable as the inland colonists. Although the beach was the first habitat to be colonized, the pioneer vascular plants there have not increased to the same extent as the inland plants.

The ocean has also been a great barrier for

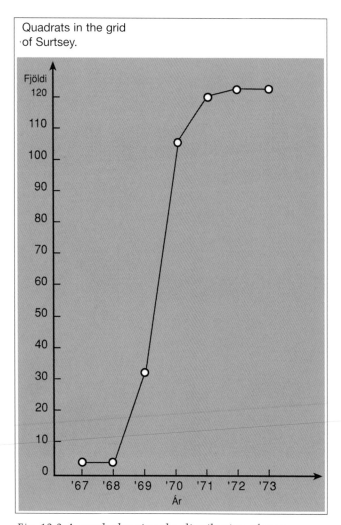

Quadrats in the grid of Surtsey.

Fjöldi

Ár

Fig. 13.3 A graph showing the distribution of moss.

small terrestrial animals that have started out on a tour to Surtsey or were dispersed in the direction of the island. For these individuals the beach was the most inhabitable area. There organic material was available for birds, various invertebrates and lower animals. On some occasions the beach has become covered with euphausids, which have been washed ashore, and which in turn have served as a food source for various kinds of birds, insects and lower organisms. In many ways the shore on Surtsey thus soon resembled any other Icelandic coastline.

As time went on various organisms, however, also started occupying the upper part of the island. An unfavorable substrate could be one reason for a slow colonization of an island. But the substrate on Surtsey per se does not seem to differ markedly from other *volcanic tephra, and plants can grow on it where water is available. This was demonstrated by moving three types of substrates, e.g. tuff, sea-sand and pumice, from Surtsey and placing these in containers with five other mainland substrates in the middle of a meadowland at an experimental station near Reykjavik. After three summers had elapsed the surface of a peat sample had obtained 60.7% cover of vascular plants that had blown in as diaspores from the neighborhood, whereas the Surtsey substrate had a 10% average cover while some cinder from the Hekla eruption in 1970 only obtained 1.9% cover. This demonstrated that plants could occupy the substrate of Surtsey if they only managed to get to the island.*

The environment on Surtsey is cool, windy and rainy, but the periodical drought is mostly responsible for the slow establishment of life on the island. As the tephra gradually hardens into tuff, its water-retention will increase and the abrasive effect of the glass particles will be minimized. This substratum will then be accessible to mosses and even grasses and to various dicotyledonous species now growing on the neighboring islands.

A common believe is, that lichens are the primary colonists of the xeric habitats of lava flows, which are then followed by mosses, and finally succeeded by grasses and dicotyledons. Such is the succession in many rock and lava habitats on the mainland of Iceland. On Surtsey, however, bacteria, algae and vascular plants preceded the colonization of lichen and mosses.

Three years passed before any moss appeared on the lava, and only after six years the lichens started to colonize it.

When the local individuals of moss started reproducing, there was a population explosion in the habitat and the colonization became quite rapid. During the succeeding three years the mosses spread over most of the lava that had a suitable environment and was not too much affected by the salt spray. This enormous increase in distribution may be measured in number of quadrats occupied by moss. In 1967 moss was found only in three quadrats of the total 240 quadrats of Surtsey, the figure had jumped to 120 quadrats in 1971. This increased distribution can be noted in the steep rise of the curve that shows the number of moss covered quadrats. This tendenesy slowed down with time (Fig. 13.3). Since then the tufts of moss are gradually enlarging and uniting in a close mat, and the biomass per unit area is increasing (Fig. 13.4).

The moss invaded the lava as a monoculture. The secondary invaders, bacteria, algae and moulds, may now be found associated with the moss, but the moss does not seem to rely on them in its establishment on the lava.

Fig. 13.4. The moss carpet being measured in the volcanic crater Surtungur.

By comparing the xerarch succession of the vegetational development on the lava flows of the mainland, it may be assumed that the Surtsey moss will develop a thick continuous carpet, at least in the centre of the lava apron and in the crater Surtungur. This moss carpet will then collect dust and minerals, and nutrients will be deposited in the dead mat of moss rhizoids, which will form a layer of humus in the juvenile soil. The accumulation of humus will then cause moisture to be retained on the lava surface. The pioneer lichens will occupy the higher ridges of the lava and gradually corrode its surface, providing better anchorage for other plants. This primary succession of moss and lichen will provide a suitable habitat for higher plants, which then, in turn, will invade the lava area.

The vascular plants have steadily increased in numbers on Surtsey (Fig 13.5). Gradually heath vegetation with the sedge, *Carex rigida*, the crowberry, *Empetrum nigrum*, and low-growing willows, *Salix* species may invade the moss carpet in the most sheltered areas. But it is highly unlikely that the island will ever obtain a climax vegetation of birch as the lava flows of the mainland, because of the frequent salt spray and heavy storms.

Particular Position of Colonists

The biota of Surtsey has been compared to that of the other members of the Westman Islands and, although it is situated farther to the south, the climate does not differ enough to cause the Surtsey biota to deviate markedly from those of the other islands, but its biota will show a pronounced difference, when for example compared to the biota of the island of Grimsey, which is situated off the northern coast of Iceland.

These two islands are the extreme outposts of Iceland, Grimsey being in the Arctic Ocean and Surtsey in the Atlantic. The Grimsey biota is Arctic and has been transported over the Arctic Ocean, whereas the Surtsey biota is more European and is transported over the Atlantic.

These are similarly the routes by which the biota has in general been carried to Iceland after the country had been freed from the ice dome some ten to twenty thousand years ago. Although Surtsey is small, in comparison to Iceland, the island may represent its southern part and the same principles of dispersal and colonization are involved. Surtsey has both the lava flows and tuff mountains that are common on the mainland, with vegetation that has undergone much the same succession steps that are now starting to develop on Surtsey.

The southern coast of Iceland has an extensive low sandy shore open to the Atlantic and is susceptible to the debris carried by the Gulf Stream. The shore of the northern ness on Surtsey is similarly subject to various drifts from the same ocean current. Although this coastal strip of Surtsey is small in comparison with that of the mainland, it is already occupied by an unusually high number of coastal species of the Icelandic flora. This indicates that the number of coastal species increases only slightly with the size of an island. It seems that an island, which has reached a certain minimal size, can actually support all coastal species available in the area, and Surtsey is definitely large enough to do this.

The lagoon, which originally existed on the northern ness, added to the diversity of the coastal habitat. The water in that pool was somewhat salty, but it has gradually filled up with cinder and sand dust. Fresh water could hardly be found. The freshwater containers, however, served as attractions for birds and these became the centres of colonization.

Fresh-water reservoirs on an island markedly increase diversity in the habitats and add to the number of possible colonizing species. It has been suggested that ocean islands can not maintain a fresh-water reservoir if they are less than one hectare in area. Although Surtsey is considerably larger, 180 hectares, it is doubtful that fresh water will ever collect on the island to any extent. There are hardly any fresh water deposits either on the other islands in the Westman Islands group. This is due to the poor water-holding ability of the volcanic substratum, a common phenomenon on all volcanic islands.

Biotas of volcanic islands may differ due to climatic differences, remoteness, diversity of available species of the source region, age, size and physiography. In spite of this difference, many of the same principles are involved affecting transport of potential immigrants, their colonization, propagation and then their exodus and extinction. Thus one can compare Surtsey with larger islands like Iceland. The development is subject to the same principles.

In the Atlantic one may compare the biota of various volcanic islands from north to south along the Atlantic ridge, such as: Jan Mayen, Iceland, Azores, and Tristan da Cunha. These islands show a marked difference in types and number of species and number of endemics, but they have in common the relative poverty of species, lack of genetic diversity in the present taxa and ecological disharmony when compared with the biota of adjacent continents. Of the 450 species of flowering plants found in Iceland there are hardly any true endemics, nor of the 45 species growing on Jan Mayen, whereas there are 15 endemics of the 124 species of flowering plants found on Tristan da Cunha.

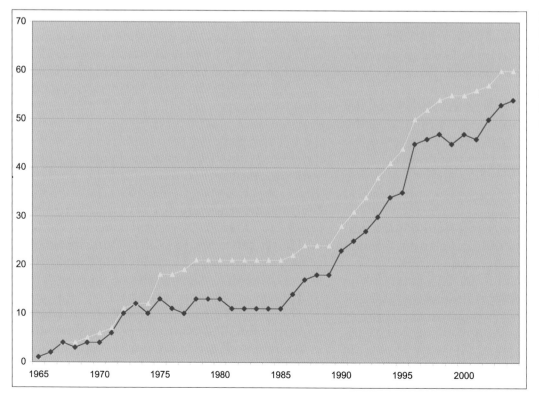

Fig. 13.5. The number of vascular plant species on Surtsey. White line is total number of plants found. Black line is number of plants alive each year.

These are all remote islands that reach an altitude of over 2000 m. They vary in size, and although the diversity of the biota of an island is, in general, directly proportional to its area, this trend is not as effective on the biota as the climate may be. Jan Mayen is 371.8 sq. km in size, compared with the 159 sq. km of the Tristan group, and has only one third of the number of vascular plants. These islands may be of similar age or less than 20 million years old, but the actual age of their biota may be highly different, as the North Atlantic islands have undergone denudations during glacial periods. Thus their present biota only dates back to the end of the last ice age, which explains their lack of endemics.

One of the factors influencing the formation of endemic species is the founder effect, where a small number of colonists on an island will contribute only a fraction of the gene pool of the source population and the random samples of migrants may not have represented the original population in genetic respects. This initial difference may result in an endemic species after an evolution of 10 million years (in Tristan) or over 10 thousand years (in Iceland), but the tendency towards genetic drift will hardly be measurable on an island after only a few decades.

Nevertheless, the first individual of flowering plants, such as the pioneer of sheep's sorrel, which has now started growth on Surtsey, may have a much greater influence on the population than possible later arrivals.

The majority or even all individuals of the future population of this species on the island may descend from this particular individual. But there will hardly occur a chance loss of many alleles in the genetic constitution of the Surtsey population of this particular species. This would be effective if the island was more remote. But chances are that many other individuals will arrive later and level out the possibility of much genetic difference in the species.

Similarly, the colonizing species may not be a random sample of the species in the neighboring community. A chance immigration of a rare species might thus affect the formation of an unusual association. This, however, is not the case on Surtsey, as nearly all the colonists are either very common in the neighborhood or in comparative habitats on the mainland such as new lava flows or sandy beaches. The colonization of the first mosses may have been somewhat unusual, but soon the most common moss species of lava flows in Iceland also dominated the Surtsey lava.

Following the establishment of a colonist and its first successful reproduction on the island, the distribution of the species in the ecosystem enters a new phase. From then on the spread of the species is subject to two modes of distribution. One is an external migration, which follows a relatively stable pattern year by year. The other is based on an internal source of diaspores, becoming increasingly effective as time goes on and succeeding generations start reproducing and forming new centres of distributions. The internal migration is characterized by a radiant spread of organisms from the source plant, forming colonies with varying density according to their processes of dissemination and vegetative reproduction.

In the Surtsey research, individual plants have been mapped to keep track of this basic development, and the structure of the vegetation as is demonstrated by the following examples.

It usually takes a *Honckenya* plant six years to reach the state of flowering. In 1971 the first five plants of this species developed flowers and one matured seeds and bore two fruits. The following year 12 plants flowered, of which 9 matured and produced 346 fruits. The seeds from both years were mostly distributed in the neighborhood of the flowering plants, some were buried deep in sand and others carried out to sea. In 1973 there were 548 plants of this species recorded on Surtsey, of which the majority may have developed from locally produced seeds. Similarly, plants of the species *Cochlearia officinalis* flowered, produced a number of seeds and gradually formed colonies that displayed many of the major ecological problems to which living beings are subject in the environment, such as competition for space between individuals and for their use of available energy, nutrition and water.

This pioneer population also showed variation in distribution and density, as well as fluctuation in the annual reproduction rate and mortality. By getting well acquainted with the productivity, life span and fate of the individual in the population, it is possible to get a better picture of its distribution pattern and even to predict its development in the ecosystem.

Comparison with Remote Islands

The difference in climate of remote volcanic islands greatly affects their biota. Thus a mild climate and very low precipitation on the Galapagos Islands, situated at equator in the Pacific Ocean, or as that of Lanzarote, the easternmost member of the Canary Islands, accounts for a slow rate of erosion and introduction of plants to its basaltic lava flow. In comparison the rather high rate of weathering and colonization of plants on the Surtsey lava is affected by frequent winds and high humidity.

When high humidity is also accompanied by high temperatures, the colonization can be quite rapid as in the case of the island of Krakatoa, which became almost completely denuded of life during the explosive eruption in 1883. Fourteen years following the eruption there were 50 species of vascular plants growing on the island. There were numerous coastal plants and several had spread to higher elevations. It has been estimated that 60% had been transported by sea, 32% by air currents and 8% by birds. But only 25 years after the outbreak the island was again covered with a thick vegetation and had obtained an animal population comparable to that of the neighboring archipelago.

The dispersal and colonization was so rapid that three years after the eruption it was too late to investigate how all the different life forms had managed to disperse and colonize the island.

In 1930 a new island was formed in the old Krakatoa crater. This island was named Anak-Krakatoa. This new island is in many ways similar to Surtsey both in size and shape. A comparison between colonization and development of life on these two islands is instructive, although they are in different climatic and ecological zones. At present a thorough study is being carried out on Anak-Krakatoa in order to follow the dispersal of organisms to the island.

Based on the study of Krakatoa, it has been taken for granted that blue-green algae are the first colonizers of a volcanic substratum, followed by lichens and moss and then higher plants. But the Surtsey study shows that many of the coastal species occupied the lava flows as pioneers independent of any lower plants, and that the mosses arrived, a few years later, although they eventually became the most active colonizers of the lava.

A similar phenomenon takes place on Hawaii, where the *Metrosideros collina* is one of the first trees to occupy the new lava, spreading its roots over its surface even before mosses arrive.

In general, the biota of an island is in a state of equilibrium when governed by the balance between immigration and extinction. The immigration rate may be high where the distance to the island is short and where there is an abundant source of species.

On Surtsey the immigration rate has been very slow compared with that of Krakatoa and many years will pass before it reaches equilibrium. The pioneer species of flora and fauna that have thus far established themselves on Surtsey are all common inhabitants of the neighborhood. Thus the island's biotic community being only a fraction of the Westman Islands' biota may to some extent be considered to be in harmony with the biota of the adjacent landmasses.

In forecasting future trends in the biotic development it is, however, reasonable to predict that the biota may become more variable on Surtsey than on many other members of the Westman Islands, due to its greater size and diversity in topography. Many of the Westman Islands are mere stacks with sheer cliffs, whereas Surtsey has low beaches. The Surtsey coasts will, however, steadily erode and high sea cliffs will eventually be formed similar to those found on its neighboring islands.

More remote in time is a possible extinction of species from Surtsey. This may take place when the lava becomes completely covered with grasses and angelica succeeding the pioneer mosses and lichens and has developed a heavy carpet of

Fig. 13.6. A young gannet on Súlnasker that is a rock island close to Surtsey, watches the volcanic area, which eventually will be the home of gannets, when Surtsey has become a mere pillar with sheer cliffs.

red fescue upon the top of the island, preventing growth of most other vascular plants. This vegetation will in turn be excavated by puffins or again denuded by the rich guano deposits of the gannets, which may eventually colonize Surtsey as it has done on the neighboring islands.

Finally, the shores may have undergone such drastic erosions, that the low sandy beaches have been cut away and the coast transformed into the steep cliffs that are so common on the outer islands. This takes place simultaneously with an extinction of the coastal plants that so far have been the main immigrants of higher plants on Surtsey. At that time the exodus will be faster than the immigration of species. The cliffs made of palagonite tuff will last longer than the lava and will serve as breeding grounds for various sea birds that will occupy the island during the summer. On the barren rock summits, colonies may be established by the stately gannet, the queen of the outer islands (Fig. 13.6). This will last for some thousand years until the cliff falls apart in one of the earthquakes or when the waves succeed in collapsing an isolated, weather-beaten rock way out in the ocean. Then the last remnants of Surtsey will disappear, and the foundations of the island vanish below the surface of the sea.

Acknowledgement

The subject of this book particularly concerns the study of terrestrial life on Surtsey during the first 40 years of the island's existence. The text is partly based on my following books: Surtsey 1994, in Icelandic and Evolution of life on a volcanic island, written in English, and published by Butterworths in London, 1975. Some of the chapters in that book have been left out, whereas other subjects have been added to describe more recent studies and their results.

In 1964 shortly after the formation of Surtsey I had decided to try to follow the first steps of the colonization of life on the island and the possible succession of communities. Although I originally started studying the development of life on the island and have partly continued the research for the past 40 years, the results presented here are nevertheless based on the work of several scientists from various disciplines, whose valuable investigations have broadened the general knowledge of these natural phenomena.

These scientific results have, in general, appeared in the Surtsey Research Progress Reports, published by the Surtsey Research Society.

In this book I have chosen to summarize some of the various results obtained from this research work without directly quoting each time the name of the scientist and author concerned, but I have listed the references of each chapter. This should facilitate further reading of the original study. I am indebted to many of my colleagues who have assisted me in the writing of this book. Scientists in various fields have given me many a good advice and looked over the text in some chapters. I am also particularly grateful to Embla Thórsdóttir and my wife Sigrún Laxdal for assisting me with the English text and to Stephanie Olsen for a helpful criticism.

The main part of this book, however, is a report of my studies as well as those of my assistants, who have done most of the routine field work on which are based the vegetation maps and various floral lists. I am particularly grateful to my assistants for their contribution to the Surtsey research project. Without their skillful observations and expedient means of tackling new problems under often highly difficult circumstances this work would not have been accomplished.

Many persons and organizations are to be thanked for valuable assistance but especially the Icelandic Coast Guard that from the start of the eruption and ever since have often given the scientists a smooth transportation to the island.

The construction of the scientists' hut has greatly improved research facilities on the island. With changes in the islands topography threatening the first building, a new hut had to be erected at a more secure location. This was supervised by The Surtsey Research Society, which has also organized various expeditions to the island. To finance these activities the Society has received support from the Icelandic State as well as foreign grants. This has facilitated the research on Surtsey. Several Icelandic research institutes have also supported the study. Some of the scientists have furthermore received various grants for the Surtsey study from both local and foreign sources.

I have attempted to present a description of the rather dramatic eruption of Surtsey and to review the parts played by the various organisms in colonization of the island by giving a brief outline of the geology and the biology of the surrounding stage. In my description of these events I have used as a background the Norse mythology, as it appears in the ancient Edda poem Völuspá, and recited in the Deluding of Gylfi written by Snorri Sturluson (1179-1241). There is an apparent conformity in the Surtsey eruption and the Nordic understanding of creation and development of life and land, and it has previously been pointed out that the ancient authors very likely were acquainted with, or had witnessed, submarine volcanic activities.

To me personally, the eruption of Surtsey and the events that followed the formation of new land and its gradual colonization by life, has certainly been a revelation. It is a unique experience to follow the creation of land and the development of its ecosystem from the beginning.

The display of these natural phenomena were so magnificent, the powers of the elements both in constructing and demolishing land so apparent, and the continuous struggle for the existence of life so fundamental, that they are bound to direct one's thoughts towards the creative forces of the universe and to the origin and destiny of life.

Sturla Fridriksson

References

Chapter 1

Introduction

YOUNG, J. I., The prose Edda of Snorri Sturluson: Tales from Norse mythology, Bowes and Bowes, London, 131 (1954)

HERMANNSSON, S., The Surtsey Research Society, Introductions in the Proceedings (1967) and Progress Reports of the Surtsey Research Society 1 (1965); 2 (1966); 3 (1967); 4 (1968); 5 (1970); 6 (1972); 7 (1974); 8 (1978); 9 (1982); 10 (1992) and 11 (2000)

FRIDRIKSSON, S., Life and its development on the volcanic island, Surtsey, Surtsey Research Conference, Proceedings, Reykjavik, 7-19 (1967)

Chapter 2

Geological notes

BARDARSON, H., Ice and Fire, Reykjavík, 171 (1971)

KJARTANSSON, G., A comparison of table mountains in Iceland and the volcanic island of Surtsey off the south coast of Iceland, Náttúrufr., 36, 1-34 (1966)

KJARTANSSON, G., Volcanic forms at the sea bottom, Iceland and mid-ocean ridges, Symposium, Proceedings (Edited by S. Bjornsson), Societas Scientiarum Islandica, Rit, 37, 53-64 (1967)

THORARINSSON, S., Iceland, Geography of Norden, 10, J. W. Cappelens Forlag, Oslo (1960)

Chapter 3

The Mid-Atlantic Ridge

EINARSSON, TH., The Eruption in Surtsey in Words and Pictures, Heimskringla, Reykjavík, 23 (1966)
Annales Islandici 1400-1800, Felagsprentsmiðjan, Reykjavík.
Icelandic book of settlement
Lögmannsannáll
Páls saga biskups

THORARINSSON, S., Surtsey, the new island in the North Atlantic, Almenna Bókafélagid, Reykjavík, 63 (1964)

Chapter 4

The eruption starts

EINARSSON, TH., Studies of temperature, viscosity, density and some types of materials produced in the Surtsey eruption, Surtsey Res. Progr. Rep., 2,163-179 (1966)

EINARSSON, TH., The Eruption in Surtsey in Words and Pictures, Heimskringla, Reykjavík, 23 (1966)

EINARSSON, TH., Der Surtsey Ausbruch, Natunviss Rundschau, 20, 239-247 (1967)

Nimbus. Earth Resources Observations, Technical Report No.2, National Aeronautic Space Administration, 69-72 (1971)
The Best of Nimbus, National Aeronautic and Space Administration, 83 (1971)

THORARINSSON, S., Surtsey island born of fire, National Geographic Magazine, 127, No.5 (1965)

THORARINSSON, S., The Surtsey eruption. Course of events and the development of Surtsey and other new islands, Surtsey Res. Progr. Rep. 2, 77-87 (1966)

THORARINSSON, S., Review of geological and geophysical research connected with the Surtsey eruption, Surtsey Research Conference Proceedings, Reykjavík, 20-29 (1967)

THORARINSSON, S., The Surtsey Eruption. Course of events during the year 1966, Surtsey Res. Progr. Rep., 3, 84-92 (1967)

THORARINSSON, S., Surtsey, the new island in the North Atlantic, Viking Press, New York (1967)

THORARINSSON, S., Island is born (excerpt from above), Reader's Digest, 92, Feb. 146-153 (1968)

THORARINSSON, S., The Surtsey Eruption. Course of events during the year 1967, Surtsey Res. Progr. Rep., 4, 143-149 (1968)

THORARINSSON, S., EINARSSON, TH., SIGVALDASON, G. and ELISSON, G., The submarine eruption off the Westman Islands 1963-1964, Bulletin Volcanologique, 27, I-II (1964)

Chapter 5

Formation and disappearance of islets

EINARSSON, TH., The Eruption in Surtsey in Words and Pictures, Heimskringla, Reykjavík, 23 (1966)

MALMBERG, S. A., Beam transmittance measurements carried out in the waters around Surtsey, Surtsey Res. Progr. Rep., 4,195-197 (1968)

SIGVALDASON, G. E., Structure and products of subaquatic volcanoes in Iceland, Surtsey Res. Progr. Rep., 4, 141-143 (1968)

THORARINSSON, S., Surtsey, the new island in the North Atlantic, Almenna Bókafelagid, Reykjavík, 63 (1964)

Chapter 6

Landscape

FRIEDMAN, J. D. and WILLIAMS, S. jr., Comparison of 1968 infrared imagery of Surtsey, Surtsey Res. Progr. Rep., 5, 9~5 (1970)

JAKOBSSON, S., The geology and petrography of the Westman Islands, A preliminary report, Surtsey Res. Progr. Rep., 4,113-129 (1968)

JAKOBSSON, S., The consolidation and palagonitisation of the tephra of the Surtsey volcanic island, Iceland, A preliminary report, Surtsey Res. Progr. Rep., 6, 121-129 (1972)

JAKOBSSON, S., Surtsey 35 ára.Náttúrufræ_ingurinn 68: 2, 83-86 (1998)

JOHANNESSON, A., Report on geothermal observations on the island of Surtsey, Surtsey Res. Progr. Rep., 6, 129-137 (1972)

KJARTANSSON, G., A contribution to the morphology of Surtsey, Surtsey Res. Progr. Rep., 2, 125-129 (1966)

MAGNUSSON, S., SVEINBJORNSSON, B. and FRIDRIKSSON, S., Substrate temperature measurements and location of thermal areas on Surtsey, summer 1970, Surtsey Res. Progr. Rep., 6, 82-85 (1972)

NORRMAN, J. O., Shore and offshore morphology of Surtsey, Report on preliminary studies in 1967, Surtsey Res. Progr. Rep., 4, 131-139 (1968)

NORRMAN, J. O., Kustmorphologiska studier på Surtsey, Svensk Naturvetenskap, Stockholm (1969)

NORRMAN, J. O., Trends in postvolcanic development of Surtsey island, Progress report on geomorphological activities in 1968, Surtsey Res. Progr. Rep., 5, 95-II 3 (1970)

NORRMAN, J. O., Coastal development of Surtsey island, 1968-1969 Surtsey Res. Progr. Rep., 6, 137-145 (1972)

NORRMAN, J. O., Coastal changes in Surtsey island, 1969-1970, Surtsey Res. Progr. Rep., 6,145-150 (1972)

RIST, S., Echographic soundings around Surtsey, Surtsey Res. Progr. Rep., 3, 82-84 (1967)

SHERIDAN, M. F., Textural analysis of Surtsey tephra, A preliminary report, Surtsey Res. Progr. Rep., 6,150-152 (1972)

SIGVALDASON, G. E. and FRIDRIKSSON, S., Water soluble leachate of volcanic ash from Surtsey, Surtsey Res. Progr. Rep., 4, 163-164 (1968)

THORARINSSON, S., The geomorphology of Surtsey, Surtsey Research Conference, Proceedings, Reykjavik, 54-58 (1967)

WILLIAMS, R. S., FRIEDMAN, J. D., THORARINSSON, TH., SIGURGEIRSSON, TH. and P ALMASON, G., Analysis of 2966 infrared imagery of Surtsey, Surtsey Res. Progr. Rep., 4, 173-177 (1968)

Chapter 7

Climate

NORRMAN, J. O., Trends in postvolcanic development of Surtsey island, Progress report on geomorphological activities in 1968, Surtsey Res. Progr. Rep., 5, 95-113 (1970)

SIGTRYGGSSON, H., Preliminary report on the results of meteorological observations on Surtsey 1968, Surtsey Res. Progr. Rep., 6, 119-120 (1970) The Meteorological Bulletin, Vedráttan, 1944-1962, Reykjavík

Chapter 8

The origin of life

ANDERSON, R. et al., Electricity in volcanic clouds, Science, 148, No. 367, 1179-1189 (1965) .

BJORNSSON, S., Electric disturbances and charge generation at the volcano Surtsey, Surtsey Res. Progr. Rep., 2,155-161 (1966)

BJORNSSON, S., BLANCHARD, D. C. and SPENCER, A. T., Charge generation due to contact of saline waters with molten lavas ,Jour. Geophys. Res., 72, No.4, 1311-1323 (1967)

FRIDRIKSSON, S., Possible formation of amino acids when molten lava comes in contact with water, Surtsey Res. Progr. Rep., 4, 23-29 (1968)

PONNAMPERUMA, C., YOUNG, R. S. and CAREN, L. D., Some chemical and microbiological studies of Surtsey, Surtsey Res. Progr. Rep., 3, 70-80 (1967)

SIGVALDASON, G. E. and ELlSSON, G., Report on collection and analysis of volcanic gases from Surtsey, Surtsey Res. Progr. Rep., 2, 93-97 (1966)

SIGVALDASON, G. E. and ELlSSON, G., Sampling and analysis of volcanic gases in Surtsey in 1966, Surtsey Res. Progr. Rep., 3, 96-98 (1967)

SIGVALDASON, G. E. and ELlSSON, G., Sampling and analysis of volcanic gases at Surtsey, Surtsey Research Conference, Proceedings, Reykjavik, 69-70 (1967)

SIGVALDASON, G. E. and ELlSSON, G., Collection and analysis of volcanic gases at Surtsey, Surtsey Res. Progr. Rep., 4, 161-163 (1968)

STEFANSSON, U., Influence of the Surtsey eruption on the nutrient content of the surrounding seawater, Sears Foundation: J. Marine Res., 24, No.2, 141-268 (1966)

Chapter 9

Ecological aspects

FRIDRIKSSON, S., On the immigration of the Icelandic flora, Nátturufr., 32, 175-189 (1962)

LOVE, A. and LOVE, D., Studies on the origin of the Icelandic flora, Rit Landbún., B-2, 29 (1947)

STEINDORSSON, S, On the age and immigration of the Icelandic flora, Societas Scientiarum Islandica Rit, 35, 157 (1962)

Chapter 10

Ways of dispersal

EINARSSON, E., On dispersal of plants to Surtsey, Surtsey Res. Progr. Rep., 2, 19-21 (1968)

FRIDRIKSSON, S., The possible oceanic dispersal of seed and other plant parts to Surtsey, Surtsey Res. Progr. Rep., 2, 56-62 (1966)

FRIDRIKSSON, S., Source and dispersal of plants to Surtsey, Surtsey Research Conference, Proceedings, Reykjavík, 45-50 (1967)

FRIDRIKSSON, S., Records of drifted plant parts on Surtsey in 1968, Surtsey Res. Progr. Rep., 5,15-18 (1970)

FRIDRIKSSON, S., Seed dispersal by snow buntings in 1968, Surtsey Res. Progr. Rep., 5, 18-20 (1970)

FRIDRIKSSON, S, Diaspores which drifted to Surtsey 1969, Surtsey Res. Progr. Rep., 6, 23-24 (1972)

FRIDRIKSSON, S., Mermaids purses as dispersers of seed, Surtsey Res. Progr. Rep., 6, 24-27 (1972)

FRIDRIKSSON, S. and JOHNSEN, B., Records of drifted plant parts in Surtsey 1967, Surtsey Res. Progr. Rep., 4, 39-41 (1968)

FRIDRIKSSON, S. and SIGURDSSON, H., Dispersal of seed by snow buntings to Surtsey in 1967, Surtsey Res. Progr. Rep., 4, 43-49 (1968) also in Plants and Gardens (Brooklyn Botanic Garden Recorts), 25, No.4, 54 (1969-70)

MAGNUSSON, B and MAGNUSSON, S. H. Vegetation succession on Surtsey, Iceland, during 1990-1998 under the influence of breeding gulls. Surtsey Res., 11, 9-20 (2000)

Chapter 11

Marine research

Marine algae

HALLSSON, S., Preliminary study of the development of population of marine algae on stones transferred from Surtsey to Heimaey 1965, Surtsey Res. Progr. Rep., 2, 31-33 (1966)

JONSSON, S, Biologie Marine, le commencement du peuplement benthique des côtes rocheuses du Surtsey, la nouvelle île volcanique dans l' Atlantique Nord, C. R. Acad. Sci., Paris, 262, 915—918 (1966)

JONSSON, S, Initial settlement of marine benthic algae on the rocky shore of Surtsey, the new volcanic island in the North Atlantic, Surtsey Res. Progr. Rep., 2,35-44 (1966)

JONSSON, S., Premiere sequences du peuplement algal sur les côtes de Surtsey, Surtsey Research Conference, Proceedings, Reykjavik, 52-53 (1967)

JONSSON, S, Further settlement of marine benthic algae on the rocky shore of Surtsey, Surtsey Res. Progr. Rep., 3, 46-56 (1967)

JONSSON, S., Survey on the intertidal and subtidal algae in Surtsey in 1967, Surtsey Res. Progr. Rep., 4, 67-73 (1968)

JONSSON, S, Meeresalgen als Erstbesiedler der Vulkaninsel Surtsey, Schr. Naturw. Ver. Schlesw.-Holst., Sonderband, 21-28 (1970)

JONSSON, S., Studies of the colonization of marine benthic algae at Surtsey in 1968, Surtsey Res. Progr. Rep., 5, 42-52 (1970)

JONSSON, S., Marine benthic algae recorded in Surtsey during the field seasons of 1969 and 1970, Surtsey Res. Progr. Rep., 6, 75-77 (1972)

JONSSON, S. and GUNNARSSON, K., Seaweed colonization at Surtsey, the volcanic island south of Iceland. Surtsey Research 11, 59-68 (2000)

JONSSON, S. and GUNNARSSON, K., Botn_örungar í sjó vi_ Ísland: Greiningalykill. Hafrannsóknir 15, 5-94. Reykjavík (1978)

JONSSON, S. and GUNNARSSON, K., Marin algal colonization at Surtsey. Surtsey Res. Progr. Rep., 9, 33-45 (1985)

JONSSON, S., GUNNARSSON, K. and BRIANE, J. P. Évolution de la nouvelle flore marine de l'île volcanique de Surtsey, Islande. Jour. Marine Res. Inst., Reykjavík 10, 1-30 (1987)

Marine fauna

GALAN, A. Benthic Amphipoda and Isopoda (Crustacea) from the sublittoral zone off Surtsey and Heimaey south of Iceland. Surtsey Research 11, 89-96 (2000)

GUDMUNDSSON, F. and INGOLFSSON, A., Goose barnacles (Lepas spp.) on Surtsey pumice, Náttúrufr., 37, No. 3-4, 222-235 (1967)

GUDMUNDSSON, F. and INGOLFSSON, A., Goose barnacles (Lepas spp.) on Surtsey pumice, Surtsey Res. Progr. Rep., 4, 57-60 (1968)

HAUKSSON, E., A survey of the subtidal fauna of Surtsey, Iceland in 1974, Surtsey Res. Progr. Rep. 9, 59-61 (1982)

HAUKSSON, E., Studies of the subtidal fauna of Surtsey in 1980 to 1987 and changes in subtidal fauna from 1964 to 1987, Surtsey Res. Progr. Rep. 10, 33-42 (1993)

HAUKSSON, E., A survey of the benthic coastal fauna of Surtsey, Iceland in 1997, Surtsey Research 11, 85-88 (2000)

NICOLAISEN, W., Studies of bottom animals around Surtsey, Surtsey Research Conference, Proceedings, Reykjavík, 34-35 (1967)

NICOLAISEN, W, Marine biological studies around Surtsey, Surtsey Res. Progr. Rep., 3, 68-69 (1967)

NICOLAISEN, W., Marine biological studies of the sub-littoral bottoms around Surtsey, Surtsey Res. Progr. Rep., 4, 89–94 (1968)

NICOLAISEN, W, Studies of the sub-littoral fauna of Surtsey in 1968, Surtsey Res. Progr. Rep., 5, 63-67 (1970)

SIGURDSSON, A., Report on the marine biological survey around and on Surtsey. Surtsey Res. Progr. Rep., 1, 23-25 (1965)

SIGURDSSON, A., The coastal invertebrate fauna of Surtsey and Vestmannaeyjar, Surtsey Res. Progr. Rep., 4, 95-107 (1968)

SIGURDSSON, A., The benthonic coastal fauna of Surtsey in 1968, Surtsey Res. Progr. Rep., 70-78 (1970)

SIGURDSSON, A., The benthic coastal fauna of Surtsey in 1969, Surtsey Res. Progr. Rep., 6, 91-97 (1972)

SIGURDSSON, A., Report on the sampling of the benthic fauna of Surtsey 1970, 1971 and 1974. Surtsey Res. Progr. Rep., 7, 20-21 (1974)

SIGURDSSON, A., A survey of the benthic coastal fauna of Surtsey in 1992 and a comparison with earlier data, Surtsey Research 11, 75-83 (2000)

SKULADOTTIR, U., Report on the marine biological survey around and on Surtsey, Surtsey Res. Progr. Rep., 2, 67-73 (1966)

Chapter 12

Terrestrial research

Bacteria and moulds

BROCK, T. D., Microbial life on Surtsey, Surtsey Res. Progr. Rep., 2, 9-13 (1966)

BROCK, T. D. and BROCK, M. L., Progress report on microbiological studies on Surtsey and the Icelandic mainland, Surtsey Res. Progr. Rep., 3, 6-12 (1967)

BROCK, T. D., Microbiological observations on Surtsey 1970, Surtsey Res. Progr. Rep., 6, II-14 (1972)

KOLBEINSSON, A. and FRIDRIKSSON, S., Studies of microorganisms on Surtsey, 1965-1966, Surtsey Research Conference, Proceedings, Reykjavik, 37-44 (1967)

KOLBEINSSON, A. and FRIDRIKSSON, S., A preliminary report on studies of microorganisms on Surtsey, Surtsey Res. Progr. Rep., 3, 57-58 (1967)

KOLBEINSSON, A. and FRIDRIKSSON, S., Report on studies of micro-organisms on Surtsey, 1967, Surtsey Res. Progr. Rep., 4, 75-76 (1968)

PONNAMPERUMA, C., YOUNG, R. S. and CAREN, L. D., Some chemical and microbiological studies of Surtsey, Surtsey Res. Progr. Rep., 3, 70—80 (1967)

SCHWARTZ, W. and SCHWARTZ, A., Microbial activity on Surtsey, Surtsey Res. Progr. Rep., 6, 90-91 (1972)

SCHWARTZ, W. and SCHWARTZ, A., Geomikrobiologische Untersuchungen, Zeitschrift fur Allg. Mikrobiologie, 12, 287-300 (1972)

Algae

CASTENHOLZ, R. W., The occurrence of the thermophilic blue-green algae, Mastigocladus laminosus, on Surtsey in 1970, Surtsey Res. Progr. Rep., 6, 14-20 (1972)

BEHRE, K. and SCHWABE, G. H., Algenbefunde in den Kraterraumen auf Surtsey, Island, Sommer 1968, Vorlaufinge Mitteilung aus dem Max-Planck-Institut fur Limnologie, Plon (1969)

BEHRE, K. and SCHWABE, G. H., Auf Surtsey, Island im Sommer 1968 nachgewiesene nicht marine Algen, Schr. Naturw. Ver. Schlesw.-Holst., Sonderband, 31-100 (1970)

HENRIKSSON, E., HENRIKSSON, L. E. and PEJLER, B., Nitrogen fixation by blue-green algae on the island of Surtsey, Iceland, Surtsey Res. Progr. Rep., 6, 66-69 (1972)

SCHWABE, G. H. On the algae settlement in craters on Surtsey during summer 1968, Surtsey Res. Progr. Rep., 5, 68-70 (1970)

SCHWABE, G. H., Pioniere der Besiedlung auf Surtsey, Umschau in Wissenschaft una Technik, 51-52 (1969)

S CHWABE, G. H., Blaualgen und Vorstufen der Bodenbildung auf vulkanischem Substrat, Bisherige Befunde auf Surtsey, Island, Mitt. Dtsch. Bodenkundl. Ges., 10, 198-199 (1970)

SCHWABE, G. H., Blue-green algae as pioneers on post volcanic substrate, Surtsey, Iceland, Proc. 1st. Internat. Symp. on Taxonomy and Biology of Blue-green Algae, Madras (1970)

SCHWABE, G. H., Zur Ökogenese auf Surtsey, Schr. Natunv. Ver. Schlesw.-Holst., Sonderband, 101-120 (1970)

SCHWABE, G. H., Surtsey, Kosmos, 67, 489-497 (1971)

S CHWABE, G. H. Die Ökogenese im terrestrichen Bereich postvulkanischer Substrate, Schematische Obersicht bisheriger Befunde auf Surtsey, Island, Pcterm. Geograph. Mitt, 4, 168-173 (1971)

SCHWABE, G. H. and BEHRE, K., On the colonization of the volcanic island Surtsey, Schweiz. Zeitschr. Hydrol., 32, 32-487 (1970)

SCHWABE, G. H. and BEHRE, K., Ökogenese der Insel Surtsey 1968-1970, Naturwiss. Resch., 24, 513-519 (1971)

SCHWABE, G. H. and BEHRE, K., Algae on Surtsey in 1969-1970, Surtsey Res. Progr. Rep., 6, 85-90 (1972)

Lichens

KRISTINSSON, H., New plant species colonize Surtsey, Nátturufr., 37, 105-111 (1968)

KRISTINSSON, H., Invasion of terrestrial plants on the new volcanic island Surtsey, Ecology and reclamation of devastated land, Proc. Internat. Symp. Pennsylvania State Univ., London, 253-270 (1969)

KRISTINSSON, H., Flechtenbesiedlung auf Surtsey, Schr. Naturw. Ver. Schlesw.-Holst., Sonderband, 29—30 (1970)

KRlSTINSSON, H., Report on lichenological work on Surtsey and in Iceland, Surtsey Res. Progr. Rep., 5, 52-53 (1970)

KRISTINSSON, H., Studies on lichen colonization in Surtsey 1970, Surtsey Res. Proxy. Rep., 6, 77-78 (1972)

KRISTINSSON, H., Lichen colonization in Surtsey 1971-73. Surtsey Res. Progr. Rep. 7, 9-16 (1974)

Mosses

BJARNASON, A. H. and FRIDRIKSSON, S., Moss on Surtsey, summer 1969, Surtsey Res. Progr. Rep., 6, 9-11 (1972)

JOHANNSSON, B., Bryological observation on Surtsey, Surtsey Res. Progr. Rep., 4, 61 (1968)

JÓHANNSSON,B. Fjölrit Náttúrufræ_istofnunar 35, Reykjavik (1985)

MAGNUSSON,S and FRIDRIKSSON, S., Moss vegetation on Surtsey. Surtsey Res. Progr. Rep. 7, 45-57 (1974)

Vascular plants

EINARSSON, E., The colonization of Surtsey, the new volcanic island by vascular plants, Aquilo, Ser. Botanica, 6, Societas Amicorum Naturae Ouluensis, 172-182 (1967)

EINARSSON, E., Comparative ecology of colonising species of vascular plants, Surtsey Res. Progr. Rep., 3, 13-16 (1967)

ElNARSSON, E., Comparative ecology of colonising species of vascular plants, Surtsey Res. Progr. Rep., 4, 9-21 (1968)

EINARSSON, E.. Invasion of terrestrial plants on the new volcanic island Surtsey. Ecology and reclamation of devastated land. Proc. Internat. Symp. Pennsylvania State Univ., London, 253- 270 (1973).

FRIDRIKSSON, S., The first species of higher plants in Surtsey, the new volcanic island, Nátturufr., 35, 97-102 (1965)

FRIDRIKSSON, S., The pioneer species of vascular plants in Surtsey *Cakile edentula*, Surtsey Res. Progr. Rep., 2, 63-65 (1966)

FRIDRIKSSON, S., A second species of vascular plants discovered in Surtsey, Surtsey Res. Progr. Rep., 3, 17-19 (1967); also Náttúrufr., 36, 157-158 (1966)

FRIDRIKSSON, S., Life and its development on the volcanic island, Surtsey. Surtsey Research Conference, Proceedings, Reykjavik, 7-19 (1967).

FRIDRIKSSON, S., Life arrives on Surtsey. New Scientist 37 (590), 684-687 (1968).

FRIDRIKSSON, S., La vie s'înstalle sur la nouvelle ile de Surtsey Science Progrès, La Nature. Oct - No 3402, 386-390 (1968).

FRIDRIKSSON, S., Life comes to Surtsey. Icelandic Review 4, 163-164 (1968).

FRIDRIKSSON, S., La vita arriva su Surtsey. Sapere 70 (709), 26-30 (1969).

FRIDRIKSSON, S., The colonization of vascular plants on Surtse in 1968. Surtsey Res. Progr. Rep. 5, 10-14 (1970).

FRIDRIKSSON, S., Colonization of life on a remote island. NAS Technical Memorandum X-62, 009, 20-22 (1971).

FRIDRIKSSON, S., Surtsey. Evolution of life on a volcanic islar Butterworths, London and Halsted Press, New York, 198 (1975).

FRIDRIKSSON, S., Vascular plants on Surtsey 1971-1976. Surt. Res. Progr. Rep. 8, 9-24 (1978).

FRIDRIKSSON, S., Vascular plants on Surtsey 1977-1980. Surtsey Res. Progr. Rep. 9, 46-58 (1982).

FRIDRIKSSON, S., Life developes on Surtsey. Endeavour, New Series 6, 3, 100-107 (1982).

FRIDRIKSSON, S., Surtsey. Two decades later. Icelandic Review 4, 18-25 (1984)

FRIDRIKSSON, S., Plant colonization of a volcanic island, Surtsey, Iceland. Arctic and Alpine Research 19, 425-431 (1987)

FRIDRIKSSON, S., The volcanic island of Surtsey, Iceland, quarter-century after it "rose from the sea". Environmental Conservation 16, 2,157-162 (1989)

FRIDRIKSSON, S., Vascular plants on Surtsey 1981-1990. Surtsey Res. Progr. Rep. 10, 17-30 (1992)

FRIDRIKSSON, S., Surtsey, Lífríki í mótun. Hi_ íslenska Náttúrufræ_ifélag-Surtseyjarfélagi_, Reykjavík (1994)

FRIDRIKSSON,S., Vascular plants on Surtsey, Iceland, 1991-1998, Surtsey Research, 11, 21-28 (2000)

FRIDRIKSSON, S. and JOHNSEN, B., The colonization of vascular plants on Surtsey in 1967. Surtsey Res. Progr. Rep. 4, (1968).

FRIDRIKSSON, S., BJARNASON, A. H. and SVEINBJORNSSON, B., Vascular plants in Surtsey 1969, Surtsey Res. Progr. Rep., 6, 30-34 (1972)

FRIDRIKSSON, S. and MAGNUSSON, B., Development of the ecosystem on Surtsey with reference to Anak Krakatau. GeoJournal 28 (2), 287-291 (1992)

FRIDRIKSSON, S., SVEINBJORNSSON, B. and MAGNUSSON, S, Vegetation on Surtsey summer 1970, Surtsey Res. Progr. Rep., 6, 54-60 (1972)

MAGNUSSON, B. Soil respiration on the volcanic island Surtsey, Iceland in 1987 in relation to vegetation. Surtsey Res. Progr. Rep. 10,9-16 (1992).

MAGNUSSON, B and MAGNUSSON, S. H. Vegetation succession on Surtsey, Iceland, during 1990-1998 under the influence of breeding gulls. Surtsey Res., 11, 9-20 (2000)

Microfauna

HOLMBERG, O. and PEJLER, B., On the terrestrial microfauna of Surtsey during the summer 1970 Surtsey Res. Progr. Rep., 6, 69-73 (1972)

SMITH, H. G., An analysis of Surtsey substratum for Protozoa, Surtsey Res. Progr. Rep., 5, 78-80 (1970)

The freshwater biota

MAGUIRE, B., jr., The early development of freshwater biota on Surtsey, Surtsey Res. Progr. Rep., 4, 83-88 (1968)

MAGUIRE, B., jr., Surtsey's freshwater biota after 14 months, Surtsey Res. Progr. Rep., 5, 63-68 (1970) 134

Terrestrial invertebrates

BÖDVARSSON, H. The Collembola of Surtsey, Iceland. Surtsey Res. Progr. Rep., 9, 63-67 (1982)

GJELSTRUP, P. Soil mite and collembolans on Surtsey, Iceland, 32 years after the eruption. Surtsey Res. 11, 43-50 (2000)

LINDROTH, C. H., ANDERSON, N. and BÖDVARSSON, H., Report on the Surtsey investigation in 1965, Terrestrial invertebrates, Surtsey Res. Progr. Rep., 2, 15-17 (1966)

LINDROTH, C. H., Terrestrial invertebrates, Surtsey Research Conference, Proceedings, Reykjavik, 36 (1967)

LINDROTH, C. H., Djurvarlden erovrar en ny ö, Surtsey vid Island, Naturens Verden, 244-252 (1967)

LINDROTH, C H., ANDERSSON, H., BÖDVARSSON, H. and RICHTER, S. H., Report on the Surtsey investigation in 1966, terrestrial invertebrates, Surtsey Res. Progr. Rep., 3, 59-67 (1967)

LINDROTH, C. H., ANDERSSON, H., BÖDVARSSON, H. and RICHTER, S. H., Preliminary report on the Surtsey investigation in 1967, terrestrial invertebrates, Surtsey Res. Progr. Rep., 4, 78-82 (1968)

LINDROTH, C. H., ANDERSSON, H., BÖDVARSSON, H. and RICHTER, S. H., Preliminary report on the Surtsey investigation in 1968, terrestrial invertebrates, Surtsey Res. Progr. Rep., 5, 53-60 (1970)

LINDROTH, C. H., ANDERSSON, H., BÖDVARSSON, H., PEJLER, B. and RICHTER, S. H., Preliminary report on the Surtsey investigation in 1969 and 1970, terrestrial invertebrates, Surtsey Res. Progr. Rep., 6, 78-82 (1972)

LINDROTH, C. H., ANDERSSON, H., BÖDVARSSON, H. and RICHTER, S., Surtsey, Iceland. Supplementum, 5, Entomologica Scandinavica, Munksgaard, Copenhagen, 280 (1973)

OLAFSSON, E.. The development of the land-arthrododa fauna on Surtsey, Iceland, during 1971-1976 with notes on ter-restrial Oligochaeta. Surtsey Res. Progr. Rep., 8, 41-46 (1978)

SOHLENIUS, B., Nematodes from Surtsey, Surtsey Res. Progr. Rep., 6, 97- 99 (1972)

SIGURDARDÓTTIR, H., Status of collembolans (Collembola) on Surtsey, Iceland, in 1995 and first encounter of earthworms (Lumbricidae) in 1993. Surtsey Res. 11, 51-55 (2000)

Birds

GUDMUNDSSON, F., Birds observed on Surtsey, Surtsey Res. Progr. Rep., 2, 23-28 (1966)

GUDMUNDSSON, F., Bird observation on Surtsey in 1966, Surtsey Res. Progr. Rep., 3, 37-41 (1967)

GUDMUNDSSON, F., Ornithological works on Surtsey in 1967, Surtsey Res. Progr. Rep., 4, 51-55 (1968)

GUDMUNDSSON, F., Bird migration studies on Surtsey in the spring of 1968, Surtsey Res. Progr. Rep., 5, 30-39 (1970)

GUDMUNDSSON, F., Ornithological works on Surtsey in 1969 and 1970, Surtsey Res. Progr. Rep., 6, 64-66 (1972)

MAGNUSSON, B. and ÓLAFSSON, E. Fuglar og framvinda í Surtsey. Fuglar. Ársrit Fuglaverndar 22-29 (2003)

PETERSEN, Æ. On birds in the booklet Surtsey 30 ára. Editors: Jakobsson, S., Fridriksson S. and Hauksson, E.., Surtseyjarfélag, Reykjavík (1993)

PETERSEN, Æ. Fuglalífið í Surtsey. Surtsey, heimasíða Surtseyjarfélagsins www ni. is / surtsey / (2003)

Chapter 13

Development

BACKER, C. A., The Problem of Krakatao as seen by a Botanist, Martinus Nijhoff, the Hague, 299 (1929)

LINDROTH, C. H., ANDERSSON, H., BÖDVARSSON, H. and RICHTER, S., Surtsey, Iceland, Entomologica Scandinavica Supplementum, 5, Munksgaard, Copenhagen, 280 (1973)

STEINDÓRSSON, S., Flora Grimseyjar, J. Icelandic Botany, 89-94 (1954)

STEINDÓRSSON, S, Jan Mayen, Náttúrufr., 28, 57-89 (1958)

WACE, N. M. and DICKSON, J. H., The terrestrial botany of the Tristan da Cunha Islands, Phil. Trans. Royal Soc., London Series B. Biol. Sci., 759, 249, 273-360 (1965)

List of organism
on and near Surtsey, which are mentioned in the text

Algae

	Acrosiphonia arcta 60
kelp	*Alaria esculenta 60, 61*
blue-green algae	*Anabaena variabilis 70*
	Antithamnionella floccosa 61
knotted wrack	*Ascophyllum nodosum 59*
	Desmarestia viridis 61
	Ectocarpus confervoides 60
	Enteromorpha flexuosa 60, 61
	Fucus disticus 59
spiral wrack	*Fucus spiralis 61*
bladder wrack	*Fucus vesiculosus 59*
red algae	*Lomentaria clavellosa 61*
blue green algae	*Mastigocladus laminosus 71*
	Monostroma grevillei 61
Diatoms	*Navicula mollis 59, 60*
Diatoms	*Nitzschia bilobata 59*
blue green algae	*Nostoc 70, 86*
	Omphalophyllum ulvaceum 61
blue green algae	*Oscillatoria 70*
	Petalonia fascia 60, 61
	Petalonia zosterifolia 60, 61
red algae	*Phycodrys rubens 61*
red algae	*Plocamium cartilagineum 61*
	Polysiphonia stricta 61
	Porphyra purpurea 61
laver	*Porphyra umbilicalis 60, 61*
	Pylaiella littoralis 60
	Rhodophysema elegans 61
	Ulothrix 60, 61
	Urospora penicilliformis 60

Marine animals

acorn barnacle	*Balanus balanoides 67, 63*
amphipod	*Calliopius laeviusculus 66*
barnacle sp.	*Balanus hammeri 66*
bivalves	*Lamellibranchia 63*
blue crab	*Portunus holsatus 63*
brittle star	*Ophiura affinis 62*
buoy barnacle	*Dosima fascicularis 63*
capelin	*Mallotus villosus 66*
cod	*Gadus morrhua 66*
common mussel	*Mytilus edulis 63*
common sea-urchin	*Strongylocentrus lividus 63*
common starfish	*Asterias rubens 66*
common whelk	*Buccinum undatum 63*
dab	*Limanda limanda 61*

dead men's fingers, octocoral	*Alcyonium digitatum 63*
edible sea urchin	*Echinus esculentus 63*
glossy furrow-shell	*Abra nitida 62*
goose barnacle	*Lepas 62, 63*
haddock	*Melanogrammus aeglefinus 66*
hydrozoans	*Hydrozoa 63*
isopoda sp.	*Idotea granulosa 63*
krill	*Euphausiacea 62*
lump-sucker	*Cyclopterus lumpus 61, 66*
marine bristle worms	*Polychaeta 62*
moss animals	*Bryozoa 63*
polychaetes	*Capitella capitata 62*
polychaetes	*Scoloplos armiger 62*
saddle-oyster	*Heteranomia squamula 63*
saithe	*Pollachius virens 66*
scallop	*Chlamys islandicus 66*
sea-cucumbers	*Holothuroidea 63*
sea-gherkins	*Cucumaria fondosa 63*
sea mat	*Membranipora membranacea 63*
sea squirt	*Ascidia callosa 66*
sea snail	*Liparis 66*
sea-urchins	*Echinoidea 63*
short spined sea-scorpion	*Myoxocephalus scorpius 66*
shrimp sp.	*Eualus pusiolus 63*
skate	*Raja batis 54*
spider crab	*Hyas coarctatus 63*
starfish	*Asteroidea 63*
trumpet worm	*Pectinaria koreni 62*

Bakteria, algae, fungi

Anabaena variabilis 70
Azotobacter 69
Mastigocladus laminosus 70, 71
Omphalina rustica 69
Thiobacillus ferro-oxidans 69
Thiobacillus thiooxidans 69

Lichens

Acarospora 71
Bacidia 71
Placopsis gelida 71
Stereocaulon capitulatum 71
Stereocaulon vesuvianum 70, 71
Trapelia coarctata 71
Xanthoria candelaria 71

Mosses

Vascular plants

Terrestrial invertebrates

Birds

long eared owl	*Asio otus* 90
mallard	*Anas platyrhynchos* 90
meadow pipit	*Anthus pratensis* 90
merlin	*Falco columbarius* 90
Northern gannet	*Sula bassana* 19
oystercatcher	*Haemotopus ostralegus* 89
purple sandpiper	*Calidris maritima* 89
raven	*Corvus corax* 55, 90
rednecked phalarope	*Phalaropus lobatus* 98
redshank	*Tringa totanus* 90
redstart	*Phoenicurus phoenicurus* 90
redwing	*Turdus iliacus* 89
snow bunting	*Plectrophenax nivalis* 56, 89
squacco heron	*Ardeola ralloides* 90
turnstones	*Arenaria interpres* 90
turtle dove	*Streptopelia turtur* 89
wheatear	*Oenanthe oenanthe* 90
white wagtail	*Motacilla alba* 90
whooper swan	*Cygnus cygnus* 90
willow warbler	*Phylloscopus trochilus* 90

Mammals

common seal	*Phoca vitulina* 66
grey seal	*Halichoerus grypus* 66

Organisms not living on Surtsey, mentioned in the text

alfalfa	*Medicago sativa* 56
Arctic cotton grass	*Eriophorum scheuchzeri* 54
Arctic fox	*Canis lagopus* 48
Atlantic salmon	*Salmo salar* 48
birch	*Betula pubescens* 97
black rat	*Rattus rattus* 48
bog-rosemary	*Andromeda polifolia* 56
brook-trout	*Salmo trutta* 48
char	*Salmo alpinus* 48
club-rush	*Scirpus* 56
common groundsel	*Senecio vulgaris* 54
European eel	*Anguilla anguilla* 48
great auk	*Alca impennis* 18
house mouse	*Mus musculus* 48
ironwood on Hawaii	*Metrosideros collina/polymorpha* 100
lady's thum	*Polygonum persicaria* 56
mare's tail	*Hippuris vulgaris* 52
mountain timothy	*Phleum alpinum* 54
North-American mink	*Mustela vison* 48
puffin	*Fratercula arctica* 19
Quick grass	*Agropyron repens* 54
reindeer	*Rangifer tarandus* 48
roseroot	*Sedum rosea* 51
stiff sedge	*Carex bigelowii* 56, 97

Photographers

Illustrations

1. Chapter p. 9: Emblem of the Surtsey Research Society.
2. Chapter p.14: Based on the drawing by the captain of the hooker Boesand (Básendar) of a submarine eruption south-west off Reykjanes 1. May 1783. During this eruption an island was formed, which was named New Island. It disappeared the same autumn.
3. Chapter p. 16: Midgard Serpent. From an illustration of a manuscript from the 17th Century.
4. Chapter p. 20: Midgard Serpent. Drawing from an old manuscript.
5. Chapter p. 29: The sun turns black. Fantasy.
6. Chapter p. 34: Rocks and boulders they made from his teeth and molars. Model: The outer islands Geldungur and Súlnasker.
7. Chapter p. 41: Windbag from the map by Johannes Stabius, 1515.
8. Chapter p. 43: And when the soft air of the heat met the frost. Fantasy.
9. Chapter p. 48: The Ash Yggdrasill. A part of a drawing from an English translation of Snorra Edda, 1847.
10. Chapter p. 51: Based on a drawing by the Danish artist Ernst Hansen, 1925.
11. Chapter p. 59: Of Ymis blood they fashioned the ocean. Fantasy.
12. Chapter p. 67: Fields of corn will grow that were never sown. Fantasy.
13. Chapter p. 94: Birds on a chart of Iceland by Bishop Gudbrandur Thorláksson. Printed 1590. Also drawings of: Gangleri, Hár, Jafnhár and The Third. From the Uppsala-book of Snorra Edda.